WALKING IN THE WYE VALLEY

About the Author

Mike Dunn was born and bred in the English Midlands but has now lived in Penarth in the Vale of Glamorgan for over 25 years. He has worked for the Welsh Assembly Government, specialising in environmental and conservation issues, and has also written widely on landscape, walking, pubs and real ale. His books include *The Penguin Guide to Real Draught Beer*, *Walking Through the Lake District*, *Walking Ancient Trackways* and *Real Heritage Pubs of Wales* (with Mick Slaughter). He is married and has two daughters, and his interests include tennis, cricket and good beer. Mike's favourite locations for walking are the Welsh borders, the Hebridean Islands and the Lake District.

Other Cicerone guides by the author
Walking in the South Wales Valleys
Walking in the Forest of Dean

WALKING IN THE WYE VALLEY

by Mike Dunn

2 POLICE SQUARE, MILNTHORPE, CUMBRIA LA7 7PY
www.cicerone.co.uk

© Mike Dunn 2015
First edition 2015
ISBN: 978 1 85284 724 1

Printed by KHL Printing, Singapore
A catalogue record for this book is available from the British Library.
All photos © Chris and Mike Dunn 2015

Acknowledgements

As usual I've received a good deal of help and encouragement in the course of researching and writing this book, but I'd especially like to thank Lois Sparling and the team at Cicerone; Kevin Straw and Ben Humphreys of Powys County Council; Gwenda and Phil Davies; my wife Chris, who accompanied me on a good number of the walks and provided many of the photographs; and Helen and John Willson, who joined us on a memorable walk from Hoarwithy.

Updates to this Guide

While every effort is made by our authors to ensure the accuracy of guidebooks as they go to print, changes can occur during the lifetime of an edition. Any updates that we know of for this guide will be on the Cicerone website (www.cicerone.co.uk/724/udpates), so please check before planning your trip. We also advise that you check information about such things as transport, accommodation and shops locally. Even rights of way can be altered over time. We are always grateful for information about any discrepancies between a guidebook and the facts on the ground, sent by email to info@cicerone.co.uk or by post to Cicerone, 2 Police Square, Milnthorpe LA7 7PY, United Kingdom.

Front cover: One of the forest rides in Haugh Wood, a butterfly hotspot high in the Woolhope Dome (Walk 11)

CONTENTS

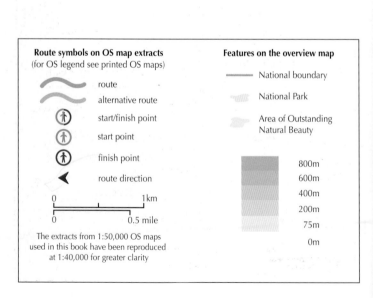

Route symbols on OS map extracts
(for OS legend see printed OS maps)

route

alternative route

start/finish point

start point

finish point

route direction

0   1km

0   0.5 mile

The extracts from 1:50,000 OS maps
used in this book have been reproduced
at 1:40,000 for greater clarity

Features on the overview map

National boundary

National Park

Area of Outstanding
Natural Beauty

800m

600m

400m

200m

75m

0m

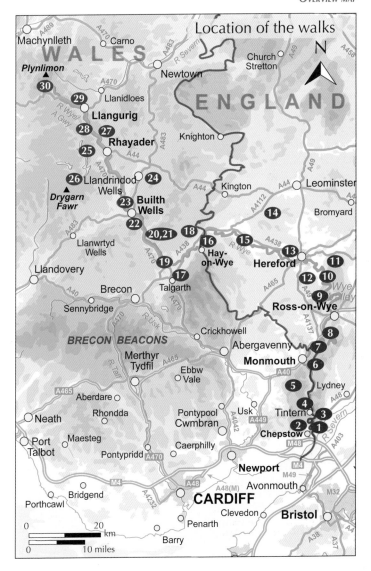

The Wye as an upland river at Pont Marteg (Walk 28)

INTRODUCTION

Looking back to Weobley from Garnstone Park (Walk 14)

The Wye may be only the fourth longest river in England and Wales, but it is almost certainly the most scenic. The author George Borrow went further, describing it as 'the most lovely river, probably, the world can boast of'. The Wye concocts a magical blend of the best of British landscapes, from open moorland in the upper reaches through pastoral tranquillity in the lowlands of Herefordshire to the final miles of its journey through a densely wooded limestone gorge to the Severn Estuary. This diversity of landscape supports a richly varied ecology, with the whole of the lower and middle Wye designated for their nature conservation importance.

It is not just the natural history of the river that is so compelling. For centuries the Wye has been a border river: in Iron Age times hillforts defended key locations on either side of the river, while Offa's Dyke was thrown up in the eighth century to keep the Welsh at bay and a string of castles sought to underpin Norman control of the troublesome Welsh Marches. Trouble flared again in the Civil Wars, when the territory – and castles such as Monmouth – changed hands several times as Royalist and Parliamentarian fortunes ebbed and flowed. More recently the Wye played a central role in the development of early tourism, when the growing

Rapids on the Wye below Wyecliff (Walk 16)

interest in the picturesque led to the development in the 18th century of the Wye Tour, celebrating the outstanding landscapes of the lower valley.

The Wye rises high on the eastern flanks of Plynlimon (Pumlumon Fawr in Welsh), the highest peak in the Cambrian Mountains, and descends some 680m (2230ft) in travelling 250km (160 miles) to its confluence with the Severn south of Chepstow. The catchment embraces several major tributaries – principally the Elan, Ithon, Irfon, Llynfi, Lugg and Monnow. But these are just the dry facts: the excitement of the Wye Valley, especially for the walker, lies in the astonishing variety of landscape experiences to be savoured as the river and the valley repeatedly reinvent themselves on the way from mountain to sea.

At first the Wye has all the characteristics of a mountain stream, yet within a few miles it masquerades as a mature, tree-lined river flowing in a wide, shallow valley past Llangurig before reasserting itself as a fast-flowing upland river from north of Rhayader to Newbridge-on-Wye. Below Newbridge the widening river flows over a rocky bed in a valley that is steep-sided at times, especially where it squeezes between the rolling upland of Mynydd Epynt to the west and the surprisingly craggy Aberedw Rocks to the east. The hills crowd in around Hay-on-Wye too, although just upstream, at Glasbury, the valley is broad and the floodplain is lush meadowland.

Downstream from Hay the Wye, now an English river, assumes another character altogether, running languidly through the Herefordshire plain past riverside pastures and, increasingly, arable fields. South of Hereford a series of big, sweeping meanders creates narrow fingers of land that are almost cut off by the broad, sweeping river. This impression of indolence is deceptive, however, for the Wye is a spectacularly changeable and at times unpredictable river, with flooding common and at times dramatic – not least in the flat lands between Ross-on-Wye and Goodrich.

Having reached the lowlands the Wye ought to wander unhurriedly across a broadening floodplain to reach the sea. But this special river has one final, remarkable twist in its tale, entering an impressive gorge just below Ross-on-Wye and flowing between the steep, wooded valley sides that close in from Kerne Bridge onwards. Bare limestone cliffs rise abruptly from the river at Coldwell Rocks, Symonds Yat Rock and the Seven Sisters, and even at Chepstow, where the river is tidal and drifts sluggishly into the Severn Estuary, cliffs rise starkly from the river to guard Chepstow Castle.

GEOLOGY AND LANDSCAPE

Superficially, the geology of the Wye Valley is very simple – Silurian mudstones and siltstones dominate the upper reaches; the middle valley is largely underlain by Old Red Sandstone; and the lower Wye is primarily a product of Carboniferous limestone, although here as elsewhere

The heather-clad slopes of Esgair Dderw, looking to Cerrig Gwalch and Moelfryn (Walk 28)

Looking across the Wye Valley to Banc-y-Celyn from the northern scarp of Aberedw Rocks (Walk 20)

there are substantial tracts of glacial and alluvial deposits masking the underlying geology.

The detail is, of course, much more complicated. At the head of the valley the broad Plynlimon massif is formed by an inlier of older Ordovician rocks within the Silurian outcrop that otherwise underlies the upper valley – including the great moorland plateau of Elenydd, which is often described as the 'green desert' of Wales. The vast emptiness of Elenydd, with its thick blanket of postglacial peat above the Silurian strata, rises above the Wye to the west, relieved only by the scattered conglomerate outcrops that form the highest summits, such as Drygarn Fawr with its spectacular summit cairns. This is Wales at its most elemental; a heavily

dissected and eerily quiet grass, bilberry and heather moor.

Some way downstream a tributary, the Ithon, hosts a remarkable landscape feature known as the Builth Inlier. The rugged topography here, with its low rocky hills, is a result of the intrusion of volcanic lavas and pyroclastic rocks into the surrounding mudstones. There are several locations between Llanelwedd and Llandegley where the rocks are exposed, sometimes with excellent fossils, and most remarkably of all it is still possible to identify an ancient shoreline with fossilised cliffs, sea stacks and beach deposits.

To the south of Builth Wells lies the area in which Silurian geology was first understood. Successive rock formations were deposited in a marine environment and are now exposed at classic locations including the lower crags of Aberedw Rocks, where olive-grey calcareous siltstones form a line of cliffs; the higher crags, with flaggy siltstones and fine sandstones full of shelly marine deposits; and the River Edw south of Aberedw, where there is an interesting exposure with signs of folding, tectonic distortion and even the ripples and scours of Silurian lake-bed activity.

As the river approaches Hay-on-Wye it takes on the characteristics of a mature lowland river, meandering across a broad, damp valley below the northern scarp of the Black Mountains. The floodplain betrays plenty of evidence of the shifting course of the river, with abandoned river channels and several oxbow lakes, especially to the west of Glasbury. The effects of glaciation are plainly visible between Hay-on-Wye and Clyro, where the river has cut a narrow channel through an impressive moraine where glacial deposits are heaped up to a height of 50m (165ft).

This impression of maturity follows the Wye on its journey through Herefordshire as a tree-lined river centred in a broad floodplain flanked by low, rolling hills. There are far-reaching views across quintessential English farmland, with the underlying Old Red Sandstone giving a characteristic rich red colour to the soils. Rock exposures are rare, but occasionally the meandering river has carved out low cliffs – for example at Brobury

Scar and at Bridstow near Ross-on-Wye. Below Hereford the meanders become more pronounced, isolating the low-lying King's Caple and Foy peninsulas.

To the west of the river the land gradually rises to the brownstone scarp, with astonishing views westward to the Black Mountains from the summit of Aconbury Hill and extensive woodlands on ancient sites such as Athelstan's Wood. To the east the uplifted older rocks of the Woolhope Dome form an area of complex geology and spectacular landscape, with hidden valleys and narrow parallel ridges. An intricate blend of orchards, pastures and semi-natural woodland typifies the area, with the nature reserves of Common Hill and Lea and Paget's Wood providing particular highlights.

South of Ross-on-Wye the river continues sluggishly at first between lush river meadows before suddenly entering a narrow, twisting gorge between high river cliffs. The rim of the plateau above the gorge consists in several places of puddingstone – a hard quartz conglomerate (previously much in demand for millstones) – which outcrops on Coppet Hill near Goodrich and, spectacularly, at the Buckstone and Near Hearkening Rock, where the breakaway boulder known as the Suck Stone – the largest detached boulder in Britain – lies where it fell just below the ridge.

From Monmouth to the river's mouth south of Chepstow the Wye

The massive bulk of the detached boulder known as the Suck Stone (Walk 6)

is confined in a narrow valley below steep wooded slopes punctuated by limestone cliffs. On either side of the river is an extensive plateau – around Trellech to the west and the Forest of Dean to the east – with woodlands and heathland. The extent to which the river has cut down through the plateau is shown by the abandoned meanders at Newland (where the misfit valley is now more than 100m/330ft above the level of the Wye) and St Briavels.

PLANTS AND WILDLIFE

In very broad terms, the Wye Valley can be divided into three ecological zones: the valley grasslands, with riverside meadows and enclosed fields; the steeper slopes on the valley sides, with hanging woods and encroaching bracken; and the moorlands above, with gorse, bilberry and occasional heather among rough grasses.

The great moorland plateau of Elenydd is characteristic of the uplands flanking the upper Wye. Aptly characterised as a vast, pale sheepwalk, it consists mostly of rank grasses with a little heather, and cotton grass and purple moor grass in the wetter areas. The mountain grazings traditionally supported the 'hafod and hendre' system of transhumance where the hafod – or shepherd's cottage – was only inhabited in summer.

In and around the river itself there is a gradual transition from mosses, lichens and liverworts higher up (especially in the gorge above Rhayader) to extensive beds of ranunculus (watercrowfoot) in the more mature, lowland river, with particularly luxuriant beds around Boughrood and near

Clockwise (from top-left): The distinctive marsh cinquefoil at Cors y Llyn (Walk 23); Ragged robin at Cors y Llyn (Walk 23); Bee orchid at White Rocks Nature Reserve (Walk 7); Heath spotted-orchid at Cors y Llyn (Walk 23)

Monmouth, while below Builth Wells wild chives dominate the banks for several miles.

In Herefordshire the Wye and Lugg have yellow water lily, water aven and great pond sedge, but the greatest interest lies in the few remaining Lammas Meadows, managed under a medieval system where stock were excluded until after the hay cut in July. Most were enclosed by 1900, but Lugg meadows and Hampton Bishop meadows still survive.

The woodlands of the Wye Valley are world-renowned, from the oak, alder and willow along the infant river to the amazing hanging woods of the lower gorge. The Woolhope Dome and Wye Gorge retain wild service trees and small-leaved and large-leaved limes – species that dominated the woods here five millennia ago – and at Coppet Hill two precious fragments of medieval woodland have survived. The gorge woodlands are of exceptional ecological interest, with limes and rare whitebeams and a ground plantlife that includes herb paris, yellow archangel and dog's mercury.

Wildflowers come into their own below Builth Wells, with meadow saxifrage and cowslips common, while bluebells, anemones and ramsons colour the woodland floors in spring and 27 species of orchid grace the lower Wye, with bird's nest and

15

butterfly orchids in the gorge wood-lands and pyramid and bee orchids thinly but widely distributed. Semi-natural grassland still clings on in the lower valley and is best seen on the Seven Sisters rocks above Monmouth, which host a remarkable assemblage of rare plants such as bloody crane's-bill and lesser calamint.

Heathland has all but been elimi-nated through a mixture of agricul-tural intensification and afforestation, but a few fragments remain – notably at Poor's Allotment north of Chepstow. Heathland restoration projects using Exmoor ponies to control scrub encroachment are gradually improv-ing the situation at several other sites above the gorge.

Fish are scarce in the headwaters of the Wye, with only the most reso-lute of the Atlantic salmon for which the river has been renowned for cen-turies reaching the shallow pebble beds around Llangurig, where the har-diest salmon overwinter and breed. Edward II ensured that his Scottish campaign in 1308 was provisioned with Wye salmon, but over-fishing and disease has taken its toll.

Trout, bullhead and lampreys join the salmon as the river flows past the confluence with the Afon Marteg above Rhayader, and there is an increase in coarse fish such as roach and dace from Newbridge downstream, but the twaite shad is the Wye's second most important fish. Like the salmon, this ancient native fish migrates from the sea to breed, its most favoured spawning grounds being the big, sluggish meanders below Hereford.

Few mammals roam the uplands of Mid Wales bordering the Wye: bea-vers were extinct by the 12th century, red deer were hunted to extinction in medieval times and (allegedly) the last wolf in southern Britain was killed in the Edw Valley near Builth Wells in the 16th century. Even the goats have gone – they grazed too destructively and there is now a sheep monoculture on the high hills.

So the higher reaches of the val-ley now see only stoats and weasels, with foxes lower down and dormice in the deciduous woodlands. Polecats, largely confined to Mid Wales by the 1950s, are now widespread. Brown hares are present but quite scarce around the Herefordshire Wye, while water voles are declining through the loss of bankside habitats and preda-tion by mink. Grey squirrels finally ousted the reds from the Woolhope Dome in the 1960s, while a few fal-low deer roam the woodlands above the lower Wye.

The big success story, however, is the otter, which was in serious decline until the 1970s but has returned to all parts of the river and its tributaries, especially the Lugg, so that the Wye population is the most abundant and most firmly established in lowland Britain. Key factors in this revival are much cleaner river water, abundant food supply and dense vegetation cover for resting and breeding.

While birds are thinly distributed in the upper valley, especially in winter, there is a surprisingly large number of species to be seen, from the classic summer triumvirate of small birds – wheatear, meadow pipit and skylark – to threatened breeding waders such as golden plover, lapwing and curlew; raptors such as the peregrine falcon, merlin and buzzard; and a large population of ravens.

But the iconic bird of the Wye uplands is the red kite. Mid Wales was the last stronghold for this colourful and majestic bird, its moorland largely devoid of heather and hence lacking red and black grouse and the gamekeepers who would kill kites to protect them. The kite's recent renaissance has been astonishing and it is now widely distributed in Wales and beyond. Most walks in the upper and middle valley will include a sighting.

Male yellowhammer on the Begwns (Walk 18)

Closer to the river itself, dipper and grey wagtail can frequently be seen in fast-flowing water, while common sandpiper and red-breasted merganser breed in secluded spots downstream from Rhayader and the goosander patrols most of the Welsh Wye. Riverside woodlands hold important populations of pied flycatchers, redstarts and willow warblers from May onwards, with yellowhammers and linnets on the commons above, while the gravelly shallows below Boughrood are colonised by reed buntings, sedge warblers and breeding little ringed plover. Vertical riverbanks here provide nesting sites for kingfishers and big colonies of sand martins.

The woodlands above the lower gorge contain great spotted woodpecker, nuthatch and treecreeper, with hobbies soaring above the Trellech plateau, while the wetter fields near

A spectacular red kite near Smithfield Farm (Walk 23)

Small tortoiseshell above Park Wood (Walk 17)

the river provide nest sites for yellow wagtails. There is an important and historic heronry at Piercefield, just above Chepstow, while cormorants roost on the cliffs here and a few pairs of shelduck nest on the riverside.

A wide range of butterflies can be found in the valley, from large heath in the blanket bogs of the Elenydd to a much wider range in the valley downstream from Ross-on-Wye – including comma, common blue, small tortoiseshell, ringlet and (in woodland shade) speckled wood – but the best sites are on the Woolhope Dome, with large colonies of the attractive marbled white around Common Hill and a spectacular range of butterflies in Haugh Wood, which is managed by Butterfly Conservation and the Forestry Commission for uncommon species such as white admiral, high brown fritillary, wood white and white letter hairstreak.

THE IMPACT OF MAN

Human activity may be concentrated in the lower valley today, but it was not always so: there is relatively little evidence that prehistoric man used the gorge (save for a few Iron Age hillforts and the exceptional bone collections in King Arthur's Cave), but the uplands around the upper and middle Wye were much more important. The lower slopes of the Black Mountains upstream from Hay contain a number of important Neolithic tombs, at Ffostyll and elsewhere, as well as the Bronze Age stone circle at Pen-y-Beacon.

Evidence of prehistoric settlement is tantalisingly elusive, but Mesolithic hunter-gatherers roamed Elenydd, and the remains of hut circles, clearance cairns and field walls suggest more intensive agricultural use by the late Neolithic era. Bronze Age peoples left burial mounds, cairns and standing stones – including the tall pillar of Maen Serth above the ancient route from Rhayader to Aberystwyth, and the high, remote stone circle at Bwlch y Ddau Faen on the high col between Drygarn Fawr and Gorllwyn.

The Romans left only a light impression on the valley, establishing outposts at Chepstow and Monmouth to control ironworking sites; a Romano-British town at Magnis near Hereford; and a short-lived fort between Hay-on-Wye and Clyro. They had an even more fleeting presence in the uplands above Rhayader, where the marching camp on Esgair

Offa's Dyke on Tidenham Chase (Walk 3)

Perfedd housed 4000 men late in the first century but may only have been occupied for a matter of weeks before the conquering army moved on.

The early medieval period saw an extended struggle for territorial supremacy in the tempestuous Welsh borderlands, symbolised most strikingly by Offa's great Dyke (thrown up in the eighth century to protect Mercia from incursions by the Welsh) but also marked by Viking raids in the early 10th century as far inland as south Herefordshire. At the same time, however, the farmed landscape continued much as before, with evidence of corn milling as early as the eighth century.

The chronic instability of the region before the Conquest explains the urgency with which the Normans exerted control over their newly acquired territories, building castles at Monmouth and Chepstow within a decade and quickly throwing up the great castles at Goodrich, Hay-on-Wye, Builth Wells and elsewhere as statements of intent as well as defensive structures. The policy was successful in the lowlands, where the Domesday Book shows that by 1086 the Herefordshire plain was settled and prosperous. Higher up the valley, however, a more fraught relationship existed between feudal lords and the hoi polloi, with the court and royal residence at Talgarth, for example, in stark contrast to the 'Welshries' in the foothills of the Black Mountains, where the lord's tenants eked out a living from working narrow arable strips and keeping a few cattle and pigs.

In the upper valley the 12th and 13th centuries saw permanent settlement encroach into the uplands as the climate improved. House platforms and cultivation ridges – for example at Banc-y-Celyn south of Builth – hint at former settlement sites, as do the later ruins of shepherds' summer dwellings, often surrounded by small walled enclosures: a good example being at Lluest-pen-rhiw on Elenydd. There was industrial activity in the mountains, too, typified by the lead mines on the slopes of Plynlimon and Drygarn Fawr, and widespread evidence of peat-cutting.

Much of the moorland was controlled by the monks of Strata Florida and Abbeycwmhir, with sheep and goats grazing the hills, their wool exported to France and the Low Countries. The dissolution of the monasteries led to the growth of country estates – at first on a modest

scale around solid farmhouses such as Nannerth-ganol near Rhayader, where the farmstead has been dated to 1555, and later with impressive houses in parkland. Holme Lacy near Hereford was built in the 1680s on the site of a medieval deer park, while the park surrounding Moccas Court was landscaped a century later by the landscape architect Lancelot Brown (1716–1783; more commonly known as Capability Brown or 'England's greatest gardener').

The industrial era saw the river at its busiest, with water power providing the driving force for mills of all descriptions, together with industries as diverse as tanning (the last of Rhayader's tanneries closed in the 1950s), cider and perry making, ropemaking and shipbuilding. The river

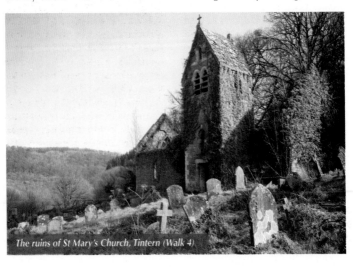

The ruins of St Mary's Church, Tintern (Walk 4)

also provided access for the industries of the lower Wye, including blast furnaces, copper smelting and tinplate works at Redbrook; a whole series of paper mills in the Whitebrook valley; and lead and copper working together with grain and fulling mills in the Angidy Valley at Tintern.

As heavy industry declined, a new source of income revived the lower Wye's fortunes. Tourists, inspired by the natural wonders of the Wye Gorge, arrived in increasing numbers from the 1780s onwards. Their arrival, often by pleasure boat as part of the renowned Wye Tour, created a slightly perverse motivation to save the decaying ruins of Tintern Abbey and much of the industrial archaeology in the valley. JMW Turner and William Wordsworth were among those stirred by the sights, and landowners responded by creating new viewing points and romantic walks above the river. The Monmouth Picnic Club went further, building the Round House on the Kymin, its first-floor dining room offering wide views over the valley to the Welsh mountains.

The early tourists' curiosity didn't extend much further than Hereford and its Mappa Mundi, however, and it is only more recently that more eclectic leisure destinations such as Hay-on-Wye with its second-hand bookshops, the Rhayader area with popular feeding stations for the majestic red kite, and the Elan Valley reservoirs have emerged as magnets drawing increasing numbers into the scenic and unspoilt upper valley.

More recent development has sometimes been less benign, although the construction of the Elan reservoirs from 1893 onwards met very little opposition, and they have arguably added a spectacular new landscape element to the somewhat barren moors west of Rhayader. The construction of wind farms has proved more controversial, but although the number of turbines is gradually increasing and wind farm development continues to gather pace, they have not yet had a profound impact on the valley, which remains largely unspoilt and perfect for leisurely exploration on foot.

GETTING TO AND AROUND THE WYE VALLEY

The Wye Valley is easily reached from Manchester, Birmingham, Bristol, Cardiff and indeed London, with the M4 providing an easy route to the lower valley; the M50, A40, and A49 opening up the Herefordshire section; and the A470 (from Cardiff and Brecon) and A44 (from Birmingham and Leominster) penetrating the upper valley. The key rail hubs are Chepstow – with slightly erratic services from Gloucester and Cardiff – and Hereford, with good connections from London, Birmingham, Cardiff and Manchester. In addition, Llandrindod Wells and Builth Wells have a few services on the

The chain ferry at Symonds Yat (Walk 7)

scenic Heart of Wales line between Shrewsbury and Swansea.

Local bus services are good in the lower reaches and, unsurprisingly, much more sporadic in the relatively remote upland country of Mid Wales, although even here careful planning will allow most walks to be completed using public transport. Details of public transport options are given for each walk, although a car is essential for a small number of the walks.

Appendix B gives full contact details of relevant public transport operators, as well as of the region's local councils. The council websites are largely focused on residents rather than visitors, but three of the region's five (for Powys, Herefordshire and Monmouthshire) offer very good public transport information, and they all feature useful sections dealing with

public rights of way, with information on temporary closures and a facility to report path problems online.

ACCOMMODATION

There is a very varied range of accommodation available in the lower Wye Valley, from fine hotels to comfortable guest houses, village inns, youth hostels and camping, but the choice is much more limited higher up the valley (with the exception of towns such as Llandrindod Wells and Rhayader). Appendix B provides contact details for websites and organisations that offer advice on where to stay and things to see or do while you're visiting the area.

While the future of tourist information centres is often in doubt because of financial constraints, the

Wye Valley is well served by TICs, which can provide information on accommodation as well as attractions, activities and events. The most useful are listed in Appendix B.

WHEN TO GO

The whole of the Wye Valley is very accessible to walkers throughout the year, with a rich variety of routes available in every season – from the crisp delights of sunny winter days to the woodlands carpeted with bluebells and anemones in spring, the wildflower meadows of summer, and the red, gold and yellow of the autumn trees. Bear in mind, however, that the high hills can sometimes be unforgiving in winter conditions, and that the Wye regularly floods in a number of places. A detailed weather forecast from www.metoffice.gov.uk can prove invaluable, and the Environment Agency's flood warnings (at www.environment-agency.gov.uk) should be checked after sustained periods of rain.

WHAT TO TAKE

The relevant maps, a compass and (especially in woodland areas and on the remote moors at the head of the valley, which have few landmarks) a GPS unit should always be carried, together with a good set of waterproofs and spare warm clothing. Don't forget to pack adequate supplies of food and water, a camera to capture the best of the scenery and binoculars for wildlife-watching. A decent pair of lightweight walking boots should be able to cope with all of the walks

Winter flooding on the Wye above Symonds Yat (Walk 8)

in this book, including the moorland and mountain expeditions above the upper Wye.

MAPS AND WAYMARKING

Walkers are encouraged to use the relevant 1:25,000 Ordnance Survey map to supplement the 1:50,000 map extracts (reproduced at 1:40,000 in the printed book and 1:50,000 in digital formats). The whole of the valley is covered by nine 1:25,000 maps:

- Outdoor Leisure 13 (Brecon Beacons National Park – Eastern Area)
- Outdoor Leisure 14 (Wye Valley & Forest of Dean)
- Explorer 188 (Builth Wells)
- Explorer 189 (Hereford & Ross-on-Wye)
- Explorer 200 (Llandrindod Wells & Elan Valley)
- Explorer 201 (Knighton & Presteigne)
- Explorer 202 (Leominster & Bromyard)
- Explorer 213 (Aberystwyth & Cwm Rheidol)
- Explorer 214 (Llanidloes & Newtown)

Waymarking is generally good – especially in the Area of Outstanding Natural Beauty from Hereford southwards – although there are some areas where improvement is needed, both to waymarking and to footpath furniture such as stiles and gates. Path problems can be reported online at the relevant county council website (see Appendix B). Where there are ambiguities or obstacles, a more detailed description

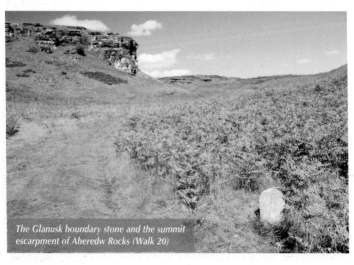

The Glanusk boundary stone and the summit escarpment of Aberedw Rocks (Walk 20)

of how to overcome the difficulties is provided in the text.

USING THIS GUIDE

The 30 walks in this book have been chosen to illustrate the exceptional variety of landscape and scenery walkers can expect to encounter in the Wye Valley. The walks are divided into four sections, starting with the lower gorge between Chepstow and Ross-on-Wye and progressing upstream to the Herefordshire plain and Welsh borders, then moving into the upper middle valley between Hay-on-Wye and Newbridge-on-Wye and finally the upper reaches from Newbridge to the summit slopes of Plynlimon. Part 1 includes walks on both sides of the gorge, visiting the picturesque landscapes around the Wyndcliff and the Kymin, and following a monks' road from Tintern Abbey. Part 2 explores the tranquil landscapes between Ross-on-Wye and Hay-on-Wye, while Part 3 tackles the more rugged country of the Begwns and Llanbedr Hill, while also visiting Llewellyn's cave, where the rebel Prince of Wales allegedly spent his last night. The varied walks in Part 4 include a trek along the Monks' Trod and a visit to an outstanding nature reserve, with a final ascent of Plynlimon to look down on the source of the river.

With few exceptions, all of the walks are well within the compass of reasonably fit walkers, ranging from easy strolls through riverside meadows to moderately strenuous expeditions

Cader Idris across the moorlands north of Plynlimon (Walk 30)

Trellech from Beacon Hill (Walk 5)

climbing the hills on either side of the valley. The exceptions are largely the walks at the head of the valley, with a couple of mountain expeditions (Plynlimon and Drygarn Fawr) and some moorland walking above the Elan Valley. None of this is rocky or exposed, but some of it is across high plateaus with few landmarks, where competence in map reading and navigation is required.

For each walk a route information box summarises the practical details associated with the walk, while a brief introduction gives a summary of the type of walk and the historical and scenic highlights encountered en route. An estimate of the time needed to complete the walk is given, although this will of course vary considerably with the experience, fitness and perhaps the age of the participants. The walk is then described in detail, with cross-referencing to the Ordnance Survey map extract provided; an enhanced description of the way forward at points where the route is difficult to follow on the ground; and notes on features of natural or historical interest on or close to the route.

THE LOWER WYE
Chepstow to Ross-on-Wye

Bluebells on the ridge above Staunton (Walk 6)

WALK 1
The Lancaut Peninsula

Start/Finish	Rising Sun pub, Woodcroft (ST 542 957)
Distance	5km (3 miles)
Ascent	110m (360ft)
Time	2hrs
Map	Outdoor Leisure 14
Public transport	Woodcroft has no public transport services useful for walkers
Parking	Roadside parking in Woodcroft

This is a short walk but one full of interest, with a sharp descent into the Wye Gorge, a visit to the ruined church at Lancaut, and a climb past an Iron Age fort and Offa's Dyke to the well-known viewpoint of Wintour's Leap.

Take the B4228 south from the Rising Sun (which has a chequered recent history and may be closed) in **Woodcroft**, passing the arched entrance to Moyle Old School Lane and then turning right onto a stony path (signposted as Offa's Dyke Path) enclosed between railings and a high stone wall. When the long-distance trail goes left through a kissing gate, go straight on under a little wooden footbridge to enter Lancaut Nature Reserve, now with the Wye Gorge dramatically down to the left. The well-defined path begins to drop steeply through mixed woodland, guided by red waymarkers and with massive limestone cliffs (used as nest sites by peregrine falcons) rising 90m (300ft) up to the right.

The Lancaut and Ban-y-Gor **nature reserves** were established in 1971 and comprise superb woodlands with oak, ash, yew and lime, together with rare whitebeams, with birdlife ranging from peregrines and ravens on the cliffs to wood warblers and gold-crests in the woods and shelduck and cormorants on the river. Dormice and the unusual lapidary snail inhabit the woodlands, while the riverine salt-marsh supports sea aster and English scurvy-grass.

The path levels out, drops steeply again and reaches an area of big, awkward boulders, which can be trouble-some for the next 50m, although the best route is indi-cated by yellow paint splashes. The hill slope above is strewn with boulders and a gap in the limestone cliffs on the skyline emphasises the damage caused by ille-gal quarrying here. On the far side of the boulders the path rises and falls through woodland before reaching a wooden bench with an excellent view downstream along the Wye, muddy and tidal here as it nears its confluence with the Severn.

Keep to the riverside path as it curves around a big meander, with Walter's Weir ahead a reminder of the former importance of the river fisheries here. When the

St James's Church is all that remains of the abandoned village of Lancaut

stark, roofless ruins of **St James's Church** suddenly loom above the path, clamber up to the right to inspect the church, which was founded in the seventh century but abandoned in 1865. The remains are melancholy but the setting above the river is superb, with a partly collapsed Norman chancel arch, gravestones propped up against the west wall and the base of the churchyard cross still visible. ◄

> The fields by St James's Church conceal the remains of the deserted village of **Lancaut**. The village was always small, with a maximum of 19 households recorded, but by 1750 it had only two inhabited dwellings – one of them the surviving Lancaut Farm – together with a cottage and fish-house below the church, which were abandoned in the early 1800s. The peninsula also housed a leper colony, although all traces of this have been lost.

The route now lies steeply up the hillside, still following the red waymarks and at first clambering up a flight of wooden steps before zigzagging through coppiced woodland, carpeted with anemones in spring, past two derelict limekilns to reach the metalled road leading to Lancaut Farm. (Slightly to the left a thin path used by climbers to reach the top of the Ban-y-Gor rocks snakes away to the north; it is worth following this for 100m or so to enjoy the spectacular views northwards along the Wye Gorge, but the path then runs above precipitous slopes and is not for the faint-hearted.) The main route lies to the right, passing the low bank defining the western boundary of the **Spital Meend hillfort** – a typical Iron Age promontory fort with low banks and ditches.

As the lane passes through the eastern boundary of the hillfort, again marked by a low bank and ditch, it becomes walled and starts to run downhill. ◄ A short section here is surprisingly suburban in nature, although there are still glimpses of the extraordinary limestone cliffs below Wintour's Leap. Go right at the main road, following this or an adjacent informal path around a

The Lancaut peninsula from the rocks of Wintour's Leap

tight bend and then going a few steps right to reach the **Wintour's Leap viewpoint**. ▶

Take the footpath angling off to the right, signposted as Offa's Dyke Path, with more views of the Wye Gorge to the right and, as the houses thin out, the broad River Severn away to the left. Beyond the enormous Woodcroft Quarry turn left by a cottage, taking a broad track down to the main road and turning right to return to the start of the walk in **Woodcroft**.

The royalist Sir John Wintour allegedly eluded his Parliamentarian pursuers in 1642 by leaping from the vertical cliffs here, although it is more likely he escaped using a less spectacular route further upstream.

31

WALK 2
The Wyndcliff

Start/Finish	Lower Wyndcliff car park (ST 526 971)
Distance	7km (4½ miles)
Ascent	175m (575ft)
Time	2–3hrs
Map	Outdoor Leisure 14
Public transport	Service 69 between Chepstow and Monmouth runs at least once every two hours and calls at the Wyndcliff car park (four buses on Sundays)
Parking	The Lower Wyndcliff car park lies immediately to the east of the A466

This exceptional walk includes part of the 'Grand Tour' of the Wye Valley, devised in the Romantic Period and beloved of artists, writers, poets and gentry. It features celebrated viewpoints and a steep ascent of the 365 Steps to the Upper Wyndcliff high above the Wye.

The way from the **car park** is very clearly signed to the 365 Steps, trending right through a quarry and then taking a path that tackles a few steps at a time as it rises through mixed woodland with a good number of ancient yews. Railings protect walkers where there are steep drops at times, and there are increasingly excellent views from Upper Wyndcliff across the Lancaut peninsula, the limestone cliffs below Wintour's Leap and the final meanders of the Wye as it approaches the wide, sluggish River Severn.

The increasingly steep ascent of the 365 Steps

A series of picturesque viewpoints, linked by romantic walks – which were constructed in the 1750s by Valentine Morris, owner of the Piercefield estate north of Chepstow – soon became highlights of the **Wye Tour**, which took visitors along the Wye Gorge by boat and carriage. Subsequent owners embellished the attractions, with the 365 Steps – a steep and rocky path built by the Duke of Beaufort's steward – and the Eagle's Nest viewpoint added around 1828.

The last part of the ascent is unremittingly steep, up a flight of stone steps that curves left and then ascending a metal ladder across a gully, and more concrete steps before the path abruptly levels out at the top of the cliff. Turn right at a post festooned with waymark discs, briefly following the Wye Valley Walk northwards, but after only 150m turn right again to drop down to the Eagle's Nest viewpoint – a platform jutting out from the top of the **Wyndcliff**. ▶

Retrace your steps to the junction of the paths and this time go southwards along the Wye Valley Walk

The Eagle's Nest boasts unrivalled views down the Wye Valley to Chepstow and the two Severn bridges. Coleridge described the view as having 'the whole world imaged in its vast circumference'.

33

on a stony track that gradually descends to the Upper Wyndcliff car park, where fallow deer can often be seen. Go straight ahead along a tarmac lane, looking down into the Wye Gorge to the left, and at a crossroads turn left and quickly left again, now using a green lane that runs past a cottage and goes over a stile. Bear right here, keeping to the field boundary, and drop down towards the main road, aiming for a stile that gives access to the A466. Go right along the pavement for 100m, cross the road with care and aim for a kissing gate on the far side of a yard. Chepstow Racecourse lies straight ahead, but turn left to find another gate in the far left corner of the field.

Just to the left are the Temple Doors – entrance pillars hinting at the location of an octagonal turreted folly known as the Temple, which was demolished around 1800 – but a superb clear path goes right, along the edge of an escarpment, with a sudden drop down to the Wye flood plain on the left. The route passes **Lover's Leap**, rising above a sheer rock face and with another dramatic view of the Wye Valley, and finally zigzags down to a junction of paths. The route heads right from here in

The view across the Lancaut peninsula from the Giant's Cave

about 1km to The Grotto – dilapidated now but once a centrepiece of the Piercefield walks, with its domed, encrusted alcove framing the view. Return to the junction of paths and drop down slightly to walk along a well-worn path that quickly reaches the extraordinary Giant's Cave.

> The **Giant's Cave** has recently been restored, although the stone giant that once guarded the entrance is no more. The views over the Lancaut peninsula and along the river in both directions are superb, and the path runs in a tunnel through the cave itself, with a big chamber and smaller ante-rooms hewn out of the rock.

Beyond the cave the way is straightforward, along a narrow but obvious path following a natural terrace halfway up the cliff but still well above the river. The way forward is rocky in places – with retaining walls on the left hinting at the difficulty of constructing the path – then crosses a stream and a boggy area before passing the gently decaying ruins of the Cold Bath (yet another feature of the Piercefield walks). ▶ A final steep climb up through the trees leads to the Lower Wyndcliff plateau and the **car park**, although the thatched Moss Cottage that once stood here and offered refreshments to weary travellers was demolished in the 1950s.

The remains of the Cold Bath include the sunken plunge pool, with some ceramic tiles still visible, and the dressing room.

35

WALK 3

The Devil's Pulpit from the east

Start/Finish	The Park, Tidenham Chase (ST 993 558)
Distance	6km (4 miles)
Ascent	90m (295ft)
Time	2hrs
Map	Outdoor Leisure 14
Public transport	Tidenham Chase has no public transport services useful for walkers
Parking	Car park on the west side of the B4228, signposted for Offa's Dyke

This is an easy and relatively short walk that nevertheless includes spectacular stretches of the Saxon earthwork of Offa's Dyke, with a remarkable view of Tintern Abbey, and which crosses restored heathland teeming with wildlife and grazed by Exmoor ponies.

Once the hunting ground of Chepstow Castle, the Chase is the most significant fragment of lowland heathland to survive in Gloucestershire and now forms an inviting and attractive recreational resource.

Go past the Forestry Commission sign for The Park at the edge of the **car park**, taking the obvious track across the open heath of Tidenham Chase. ◄

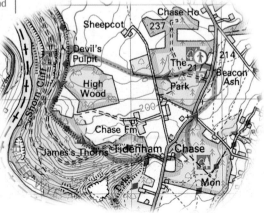

Tidenham Chase is now being actively managed to improve the habitat by restoring native woodland and clearing plantations in order to increase the area of sandy heathland, using Exmoor ponies for grazing to encourage re-colonisation by heather, bilberry and gorse. The area is now developing as prime habitat for butterflies and dragonflies, snakes, lizards and a range of birds including nightjar and woodcock in spring and summer, and crossbills, redpolls and siskins in winter.

The track across the heath soon reaches a trig point. Keep this on your left and go through a wooden kissing gate onto a clear track as far as Miss Grace's Lane. ▶ Go left and immediately right across the lane, onto a track signposted to Offa's Dyke Path and the Devil's Pulpit. ▶ An easy walk now crosses four fields, with good views to the Cotswold ridge beyond the Severn, then enters woodland again and immediately arrives at Offa's Dyke Path; 50m to the left is the **Devil's Pulpit** – an extraordinary clifftop lookout.

Despite being named after a 20th-century occupant, this lane lies on the route of a prehistoric trackway connecting the Severn at Woolaston with the Wye at the river port of Brockweir.

This route was formerly known as Abbey Road because it led towards the abbey and ferry at Tintern.

The approach to the Devil's Pulpit

37

The **Devil's Pulpit** is a spectacular rock stack standing proud from the cliff face with sensational views of Tintern Abbey (built by the Cistercians in the late 13th century) far below on the opposite side of the river. The devil is reputed to have preached to the monks from his pulpit – already known as such by 1769 – to divert them from their ways.

The route now lies south, along one of the best-preserved sections of Offa's Dyke, with earthen ramparts up to 6m (20ft) high, but now threatened by badgers and walkers. ◄ The path, enormously popular here and rebuilt with a gravelly surface, contours above the great limestone face of Plumweir Cliff, with the ancient fishery of Plum Weir far below. The trees have been felled in places to reveal views of the Wye, with the magnificent sight of Tintern Abbey the highlight. The path used to run along the top of the earthwork, with the stones used in its construction exposed and tree roots making this section tricky to negotiate, but a new path has been constructed just to the left to preserve the Dyke.

The dyke was constructed in the second half of the eighth century both as a defensive earthwork and as a show of strength, designed to keep Welsh forces at bay and protect the King's lands in Mercia.

A right turn onto a path running just below the Dyke provides excellent views of the ditch and rampart from below. The new path eventually arrives at a wide track; turn left here, and when Offa's Dyke Path swings away to the right at an informal parking area, take the very roughly surfaced lane going up past cottages to the B4228. Turn left here, then right after 100m or so onto a thin but clear path (not marked on the map, but within the open access land of Parson's Allotment, close to where Bronze Age flints were found) that crosses an open area, enters woodland and passes a few big boulders to meet a track. Go straight across here, then half-left onto another, straight track that goes through mixed woodland and then negotiates a coppice with the Church of St Michael and All Angels in **Tidenham Chase** visible on the left across the road. ◄

The land for the church was given by the owner of Chase Farm, who became the first organist; the second was her friend Miss Grace, who gave her name to the lane crossed earlier.

The path rejoins the road a little north of the church; turn right here and right again onto Rosemary Lane, where the long-lost White Hart stood in 1584 and some

Lowland heath on Poor's Allotment

surviving cottages were built in the 18th century. Quickly go left over a stone stile onto an inviting path that crosses Poor's Allotment – an open area with rough grassland, patches of gorse and bracken, and one or two copses. A delightful grassy path leads straight ahead, with the view on the right particularly impressive, dominated by the wide, meandering River Severn. The common is a favourite gathering place for winter thrushes, and fieldfares can often be seen feeding on the apple trees.

> **Poor's Allotment** was awarded in trust under an Enclosure Award in 1814, to be managed for the benefit of the poor (Parson's Allotment, on the other hand, was given to the vicar). The land was divided into animal pasture, a potato garden and allotments, with 26 parishioners entitled to put a horse, a cow and six sheep onto the pasture.

Turn left at an obvious crossroads of paths in the middle of Poor's Allotment, heading slightly uphill towards the thin belt of woodland known as Beacon Ash, and using a clear path that leads to a metal kissing gate and, on the far side of the B4228, the Tidenham Chase **car park**.

WALK 4

Tintern and the Angidy Valley

Start/Finish	Tintern Abbey (SO 533 002)
Distance	11km (7 miles)
Ascent	290m (950ft)
Time	3–5hrs
Map	Outdoor Leisure 14
Public transport	Service 69 between Chepstow and Monmouth runs at least once every two hours and calls at Tintern (four buses on Sundays)
Parking	Several car parks (some free, some pay-and-display) in Tintern

An ancient cobbled road, a deserted village, a ruined parish church and the historic industrial sites of the Angidy Valley provide the context for this walk in the quiet hills west of Tintern, with sumptuous views of Tintern Abbey as the final highlight of the walk.

This is the medieval cobbled road known by 1451 as 'the Stony Way', which the monks of Tintern used to reach their outlying grange farms to the south-west, including Porthcasseg.

From the **car park** walk past the west front of the abbey and cross the main road, taking the narrow lane uphill (signposted Wye Valley Walk) but quickly turning left along a road that crosses a cattle grid and peters out into a long, winding and stony track. This climbs steadily through woodland with a stream alongside and the constant sound of woodland birds, including the drumming of great spotted woodpeckers in spring. ◀

The track is worn to the bedrock higher up, but eventually the gradient eases, the Wye Valley Walk leaves to the left, and the way ahead lies along a holloway, badly eroded in places, running between fields and fringed with wild garlic. Go over a stile to the right, climbing up a field to cross a concrete road, and take the path signposted to Penterry Church, crossing two arable fields (the way can be muddy after rain; an alternative is to keep to the old road almost as far as Porthcasseg, then cut back to the church).

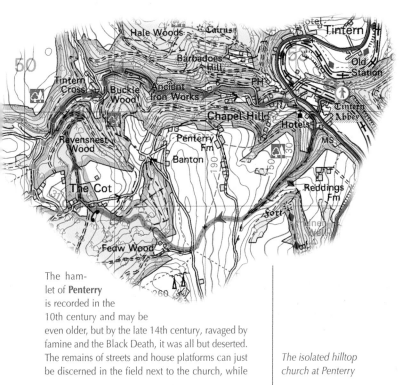

The hamlet of **Penterry** is recorded in the 10th century and may be even older, but by the late 14th century, ravaged by famine and the Black Death, it was all but deserted. The remains of streets and house platforms can just be discerned in the field next to the church, while

The isolated hilltop church at Penterry

a hazel grove in a corner of the field conceals a plague burial pit. The church fabric is largely 19th century, although there are medieval fragments and the base of a churchyard cross.

Go through the gate at the far end of the church field to cut across another field, with buzzards overhead and fine views to the Wye woodlands, to reach a narrow lane. ◀

Formerly the Roman road between Chepstow and the minor fort of Blestium near Monmouth, this was later superseded by the road through Devauden to the west, and then by the turnpike road through Tintern in the 19th century.

A path leads west from the Roman road to join the access lane to The Tout, but leave this immediately through a metal gate on the right to find a path veering left and descending gently through a big meadow, eventually running to the right of The Tout and crossing a stile to enter woodland. Go straight ahead across a forest road, taking the left-hand of two footpaths, then curve left and then right and drop down to the pleasant Fairoak Ponds, now a trout fishery fed by spring water but also home to waterbirds such as mallard and little grebe.

Head uphill on a clear track through young trees (with an understorey of bluebells in spring) then turn right on a bridleway and immediately left on a lane through **The Cot** – originally a collection of smallholdings won from the surrounding woodlands. Turn right at a red telephone box on a path signposted to Tintern Cross; this is a real highlight of the walk, through the open mature woodland of **Ravensnest Wood** on an excellent track and then through younger trees including some coppice stools.

As the descent begins, take a waymarked path to the left, but when this reaches a forest road ignore the path straight ahead (this is the direct route but sadly the path peters out after a while) and instead go left on the forest road until it reaches the metalled road some distance upstream from the hamlet of Tintern Cross. Go right along the road, passing more fishing lakes, to reach **Tintern Cross** and cross the bridge over the river – frequented by robins and grey wagtails here – to follow a lane curving round to the highest of the major industrial ponds of the steep-sided Angidy Valley – the storage pond for

The storage pond for the Upper Wireworks

the Upper Wireworks, its stone retaining walls just to the right of the route.

Immediately beyond the dam take the permitted path running alongside the stream (signposted as the Tewdrig Trail after a sixth-century king of Gwent who later became a hermit in Tintern), passing some attractive cottages on its way to the substantial remains of the Abbey Furnace. ▶

> The Angidy Valley's speciality was **iron wire making**, and by the early 17th century the wireworks here was the largest industrial enterprise in Wales, with a series of sites stretching 3km (2 miles) up the valley and some 20 waterwheels in operation. Iron ore was imported from the Forest of Dean and further afield, arriving at the river port at Abbey Mill and then being carried by packhorses to the furnaces, while packhorse trains also carried in local charcoal, which was burnt in the furnaces and forges.

The trail now winds through Glyn Wood, passing an attractive pond that supplied water and hence power

This was built in 1672 to supply cast iron to the forge at Pont-y-saeson higher up the valley, where it was transformed into osmond iron, which could be repeatedly heated and hammered to make it into wire.

The mill took iron bars from the furnaces and cut them into long rods, which were gradually hammered and lengthened into coarse iron wire.

The churchyard contains a number of significant monuments, including the tombs of ironmasters such as Robert Thompson, who built the Upper Wireworks.

to the tilt hammer mill, the scanty remains of which can be seen lower down by the stream. ◄ Keep close to the stream, with dippers and more grey wagtails in evidence, and cross a sturdy footbridge to climb up to the valley road as it approaches Tintern.

Take the higher road at a junction but then go immediately left onto a footpath alongside an old leat that runs between houses and passes the site of the Middle Wireworks near Crown Cottages, then the Bible Christian chapel, and finally the celebrated but now disused Cherry Tree Inn. Cross the valley road again to walk through the site of the Lower Wireworks – established in 1566 with four waterwheels and four hammers but now represented only by the long wall on the right.

Turn right on the main road for a few paces, then go up the lane on the right to find the former Church of St Mary's, redundant since 1972 and now a forlorn ruin, but with a spectacular view of Tintern Abbey in the valley below. ◄ A paved way leads down from the church; leave this where it bends sharply left to descend to the lane heading for the abbey ruins and the **car park**.

The impressive remains of Abbey Furnace ironworks

44

WALK 5
Trellech and Beacon Hill

Start/Finish	Trellech Church (SO 500 055)
Distance	12km (7½ miles)
Ascent	310m (1015ft)
Time	4–5hrs
Map	Outdoor Leisure 14
Public transport	Service 65 between Chepstow and Monmouth calls at Trellech every two hours (no Sunday service)
Parking	Small car park at the south end of the village

This is a very varied walk high above the western side of the Wye Gorge, taking in an ancient Welsh town, a fascinating late medieval farm complex, the waterfalls of Cleddon Shoots, and the superb woodland and heathland on Beacon Hill.

Take the lane running along the western edge of **Trellech churchyard** – pausing to take in the impressive church with its soaring spire and 17th-century sundial – and continue through a series of gates to reach **Tump Terret**, the motte of a 12th-century castle. ▶

Established by the de Clare family, the castle mound still rises 6m (20ft) and is partly protected by a ditch and outer bank. A 19th-century summerhouse built on the summit has since disappeared.

> **Trellech** was one of the most important towns of medieval Wales, with 378 burgage plots in the late 13th century, but it was destroyed by Welsh raiders in 1291 and further ravaged by the Black Death in the 14th century. Extensive remains of the medieval town, including the manor house, have been uncovered in fields to the south of the village. The stone-lined Virtuous Well, a place of pilgrimage in late medieval times, reputedly cured a variety of ailments.

A lane between holiday cottages leads back to the main road, but turn immediately right to cross a damp field, following a path signposted to **Harold's Stones**, which are only two minutes away.

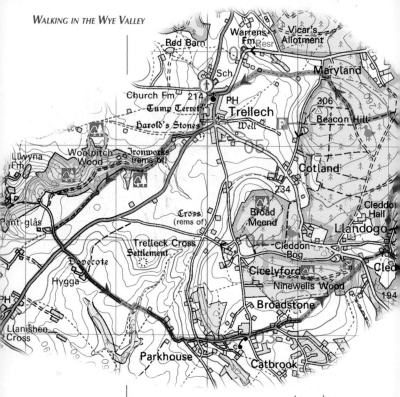

Legends associate these three **upright stones** – which are local quartz or puddingstone – with King Harold, the mythical Jack o' Kent, and with local chieftans slain in battle nearby; but in fact they date much further back and were probably erected in the late Neolithic or early Bronze Age to be used in rituals.

Go along the road for 100m, keeping straight on along a good, wide track when the road bends left. Go through a gate, then leave the main track to drop down left to cross the Penarth Brook on a wide bridge and climb to a finger-post just beyond. Turn right here, climbing a field and then skirting above woodland to reach a stile.

A permissive path drops steeply down into the valley here to visit the somewhat scanty remains of Trellech Furnace – once the site of an iron smelt mill driven by a waterwheel – but the main route continues across a series of fields above the wooded slopes of the deeply incised Penarth Brook valley, following signposts for Llanishen and enjoying views of the high hills to the west until turning left onto a metalled lane just before The Granary. Cross the B4293, making for the ancient farm complex at **Hygga**. Some of the buildings here, including barns and a shippon, date from the 16th century, and there is a striking circular **dovecot**. ▶

The origin of Harold's Stones, near Trellech, is a matter of much speculation

Beyond the horse pool a long, straight and somewhat dusty track makes for Parkhouse, with the Iron Age hillfort of Y Gaer crowning the slopes to the left and the woodlands above the Wye Gorge dominating the view ahead. A dog-leg to left and right leads to a footbridge over the Angidy Fawr – the stream flowing over the Old Red Sandstone bedrock here – and then to a climb past cottages to reach a lane next to the long-defunct Parkhouse Inn, once home to a deep-sea fishing club known as the Taverners' Angling Club. Keep ahead, climbing past the

East of the farm is an unusual horse pool, walled on three sides, into which the carthorses were led to drink and be washed down after a day's work.

47

straggling houses of **Parkhouse** and then the village green at **Broadstone**, but when the road bends right take a gravel drive on the left, going through the entrance pillars of the Woodside Farm estate.

Pass to the left of the Woodside stables, keeping on along a track and then, beyond a stile, going diagonally left across three fields with substantial stone walls and passing the picturesque ruins of a limekiln before entering sparse woodland, with the squatter hamlets of The Hudnalls on the hillside across the Wye Valley. The way lies straight ahead at a footpath crossroads, down an unexpected flight of stone steps and across a road onto a byway – very boggy for a short distance as the ground levels out – leading to a cottage on the edge of the hamlet of **Cleddon**. ◀

The philosopher Bertrand Russell, the son of Viscount and Lady Amberley, was born at Cleddon Hall (then called Ravenscroft), just to the left of the route.

Turn left onto the lane by the cottage and right onto a minor road for 100m to reach the lip of the Wye Gorge at the top of the picturesque cascades known as Cleddon Shoots. The falls are impressive after rain, and the view down through the acid woodlands to the river far below is stunning. Follow the Wye Valley Walk to the north for

Restored heathland on Beacon Hill

500m on a good track through mature woodland, but at a complex junction go left, across a forest road and past a seat, onto a narrowing but well-defined path that heads uphill for a while before becoming a wide track on the eastern plateau of Beacon Hill.

Cross a forest road, then go through a gate onto a gravelly track climbing very gradually through heathland, with heather, gorse, and naturally regenerated small trees – predominantly larch, silver birch, oak and Scots pine. ▶ Turn right onto a forest road at the John Chivers memorial bench (the path ahead quickly reaches the summit of **Beacon Hill**, famous for its panoramic views of the Wye Valley, Forest of Dean and Welsh mountains, and also for its nightjars, which can be heard churring on summer evenings). Beyond a cattle grid the forest returns, but the way remains downhill to pass a barrier and turn left, reaching the tarmac of Beacon Road after 50m.

A fingerpost just to the right indicates the return route to Trellech, first going diagonally across a series of small fields mainly grazed by horses, with the village and especially the church spire increasingly obvious. Turn right through a gate onto a gravelly track, then left to cut a corner off across a final sheep pasture and reach the road on the outskirts of **Trellech**, only 100m from the **church**.

This is the site of a Forestry Commission heathland restoration project, using Welsh mountain ponies to encourage the return of heathland species and conserve this locally threatened habitat.

WALK 6

The Kymin

Start/Finish	White Horse Inn, Staunton (SO 547 126)
Distance	8km (5 miles)
Ascent	440m (1445ft)
Time	3–4hrs
Map	Outdoor Leisure 14
Public transport	Staunton has a few buses each day on service 35 between Monmouth and Ross-on-Wye
Parking	On-street parking in Staunton village

This is a wonderful walk high above the Wye Valley, encompassing magnificent views, possible encounters with wild boar, the largest detached boulder in Britain and a Georgian banqueting house and naval temple on the summit of the Kymin.

The Buck Stone was a rocking stone before it was dislodged by Victorian vandals – a Monmouth innkeeper and his guests (travelling actors from London) – who rolled it down the hillside in 1885. It is now cemented in place.

From the White Horse in **Staunton**, head along the main road towards Monmouth for 200m, then take the curving lane rising on the left before going quickly right over a stile to clamber over rocks onto a path alongside a vividly green, mossy wall to reach the **Buck Stone** – a remarkable rock, which, at 279m (915ft), marks the high point on the quartz conglomerate ridge overlooking the Wye Valley, and which has a dramatic view of the Black Mountains to the north-west. ◀

Continue alongside the mossy wall on a path signposted as the Redbrook spur of the Highmeadow Trail. Drop down to reach a tarmac lane, with splendid views ahead of Newland Church and, to its right, the obvious course of a long-abandoned meander of the River Wye. Cross the lane to pick up a beautiful green path across the common land of Staunton Meend.

In 1629 the waste land of the high ridge, known as **Staunton Meend**, was acquired by the Hall family, owners of Staunton Manor and the huge Highmeadow estate, but 21ha (51 acres) has survived as common land with a mixture of acid grassland and birch woodland. Commoners have the right to graze the land and take turf, bracken, firewood, brush and game, but the rights are rarely exercised and conservation measures are now in place to control the spread of bracken, using Exmoor ponies.

Descend by the edge of the common land, with brambles and gorse to the left and thin woodland to the right. Pass a house and join a roughly gravelled track, turning right to pass Knockalls Lodge and go through a

51

In the 1820s the Crown Commissioners of Woods, who had bought the Highmeadow estate, planted around 220ha (550 acres) as part of the policy of raising oaks for future naval requirements, with a woodman's lodge constructed in Knockalls Inclosure.

The Naval Temple on the summit of the Kymin

gate. ◄ Swing left on a forest road after 100m, but when this bends sharply left after 200m or so, take the obvious but unsignposted footpath dropping down to the right through the larches of **Bunjups Wood**, with their superb autumn colours. Cross two forest roads and a disused railway to reach and turn right along the Newland to Redbrook road. Just before reaching the Mill Pond, which powered Upper Redbrook's heavy industries, take the track on the right (Duffield's Lane), gaining height with **Offa's Dyke Path** joining from the left.

The track passes the isolated farmsteads at Duffield's Farm and Upper Beaulieu Farm – the latter formerly part of a grange farm belonging to the abbey of Grace Dieu by 1560, but much extended in the 20th century – then forks right along the edge of Harper's Grove for the final section of the ascent to the **Kymin**. This is a delightful, easy walk through woodland, leading to a narrow lane and car park. Go straight across here to reach first the **Naval Temple** and then the Round House.

Now owned by the National Trust, the **Kymin** is an area of hilltop pleasure grounds with exceptional views westwards over the Wye Valley, the Black Mountains and Sugar Loaf, and eastwards into the Forest of Dean, but it is also home to two remarkable buildings. The gentlemen of the Monmouth Picnic Club built the Round House – a circular Georgian banqueting house – in 1794, while the Naval Temple was built six years later to celebrate the naval victories of the Napoleonic Wars.

Leave the Round House to the north and turn right at a waymark post, going through a kissing gate onto a clear path running diagonally across a field, with fine views eastwards across a patchwork of fields to wooded hills. The way lies straight ahead through a copse, across another field and then right, onto a track leading down to go slightly left across the Staunton Road. Drop down on a rocky path to reach and turn right along a forest road, going left at a junction after 200m and following the wide, gravelly forest road as it descends in a series of wide curves into a valley (a bridleway offers a steeper shortcut but is very hard to find).

Follow the forest road down the valley, with the stream to the right, until it curves left and reaches a complex junction in the middle of **Reddings Inclosure**. ▶ Turn right on a grassy track rising above the stream, now on the left, and follow this around a sharp left-hand bend. Look out for a path on the right that rises towards the edge of the woodland, with glimpses of the farmland around Conigre Barn, but on meeting a minor forest road take this to the right. The retrospective view from the top of the hill is exceptional, taking in the woods above the Wye and the imposing Wyastone Leys. Keep ahead along the track to reach the **Suck Stone**, high up on the left. ▶

Climb to the right of the Suck Stone to reach another dramatic landscape feature, the **Near Hearkening Rock**, a substantial cliff face of quartz conglomerate and sandstone, with spectacular overhangs

Reddings Inclosure holds the largest known population of spreading bellflower – a biennial herb of dry, well-drained sunny sites – in Wales.

Widely regarded as the largest detached boulder in Britain, the Suck Stone is a huge block of quartz conglomerate, possibly weighing as much as 14,000 tons, which has slipped down the hill from the cliffs above.

53

The overhanging Near Hearkening Rock

The rock's name derives from its former use by gamekeepers, who used its acoustic qualities to pick up the sounds of poachers in the woods below.

and magnificent views north-west to the Skirrid and the Black Mountains. ◄ From the Near Hearkening Rock a path runs south through the delightful **Highmeadow Woods**, keeping to the edge of the quartz conglomerate ridge, until a path rises to the left to join a forest road going right, past Reddings Lodge, and through open bluebell woodland to reach a housing estate on the edge of **Staunton**. Go straight on here to reach the A4136 close to the White Horse.

WALK 7

King Arthur's Cave and the Seven Sisters

Start/Finish	Entrance to White Rocks Nature Reserve (SO 548 157)
Distance	7km (4½ miles)
Ascent	220m (720ft)
Time	2–3hrs
Map	Outdoor Leisure 14
Public transport	Crocker's Ash, 1.5km from White Rocks, has a bus every two hours on route 34 from Ross-on-Wye to Monmouth
Parking	Limited parking at and around the entrance to the reserve

This is a hugely varied walk, with delightful nature reserves, the riverside bustle of Symonds Yat, an enormous hillfort with panoramic views, and a celebrated cave that once provided shelter for exotic prehistoric animals.

Go through the gate into **White Rocks Nature Reserve**, following the obvious path north-east or, better still, exploring the open land to the left – formerly a quarry and now a mixture of woodland, scrub and

The bramble thickets are home to several species of butterfly – notably marbled whites and ringlets – while common spotted orchids are abundant and there are also bee and pyramidal orchids in places.

The field is dotted with yellow ant mounds and supports a diverse calcareous plantlife, ranging from cowslips, early purple and greater butterfly orchids and harebells to devil's bit scabious, marjoram, pignut and autumn crocus.

grassland. ◄ When the path forks by a wayside seat take the left-hand option, passing through tall bracken that often conceals fallow deer. At the edge of the reserve turn left along May Bush Lane, a beaten-earth track, and when this reaches a tarmac road the route lies immediately right, along Horse Pool Lane.

After only 150m turn right again to follow a clear path through the **Miners Rest Nature Reserve**, taking the right-hand option and curving round to the left to reach a lane by an information board. The reserve now consists of broad-leaved woodland, but the ruined limestone walls of field boundaries can still be seen. Go slightly to the left across the lane and through a gate in the deer fence into a third nature reserve – Woodside – following a narrow path through scrub and woodland and then cutting through an old arable field that reverted to pasture some decades ago. ◄

Turn left on another beaten-earth track on the eastern edge of Woodside, and at a complex junction after 150m turn sharply right onto a good path descending gradually through the Woodland Trust's Symonds Yat Woods – a classic semi-natural ancient beech woodland. Curve right, then turn sharply left opposite some disused shafts, with even better examples of the entrances to old ironstone workings slightly further downhill at the base of a cliff. The descent steepens on an excellent track through mature woodland, with a precipitous drop to the right, before a left turn leads past an even more impressive limestone cliff and down a narrowing path to reach the road at **Symonds Yat West**.

A path to the left leads to the river and the ancient hand ferry giving access to the pubs and other facilities of Symonds Yat East, but the main route ignores this and instead keeps straight on when the road turns left. There is a choice between a sometimes narrow riverside path with good views of the rapids – scenic and popular with canoeists – and the main track, until the path climbs up to merge with the track just beyond the scanty remains of the New Weir Forge.

The ironworks at **New Weir Forge**, powered by water diverted from the river, were in operation by 1570 and included a slitting mill, which produced nails, and a rolling mill driven by waterwheels. Workers' cottages lay on the hillside above the forge, and the owner's garden and orchard lay alongside the upper path. The works were disused by the late 18th century and the remains are now widely scattered in the woodland.

Biblins Bridge, a suspension footbridge over the Wye

The stony track continues straight ahead for some distance, eventually swinging right to pass through the grassy **Biblins campsite**, with the tufa-encrusted limestone cliff below the Dropping Well to the right under the slopes of Lord's Wood, with its caves and rock shelters, and the swaying suspension footbridge – constructed by the Forestry Commission in 1957 – straight ahead. Go straight past the footbridge on a dusty track, eventually slanting left across a riverside pasture to reach the river again in the company of an excellent woodland path below the limestone rock towers of the **Seven Sisters**. ▶

Extensively quarried in the past, the Seven Sisters dominate the surrounding landscape and constitute an important habitat for rare plant species requiring lime-rich grassland.

Turn right just before a metal gate, now going steeply uphill on a tough but rewarding path through the woods. The slope eases and the path nears the edge of the trees, with a field ahead, but turn left here on a path that enters the Little Doward woodland and climbs steadily to reach a ladder stile in front of a little cliff. The way lies to the right here on a wide green path, which reaches a junction of pedestrian ways at the edge of the **Little Doward hillfort**.

> The massive **hillfort** at Little Doward is defended by steep cliffs and a single rampart and ditch. The 19th-century ironmaster Richard Blakemore, regarded as 'entirely unacquainted with the antiquarian interest' here, created a picturesque landscape with follies and viewpoints, driving carriage roads right through the ramparts. Recently the trees have been removed and white cattle now control the vegetation.

Turn right at the path junction, taking a route that runs round the northern boundary of the fort, with good views in places of the rampart and deep ditch. This is one of Blakemore's carriage drives, eventually sweeping round to the left. Turn left to walk through a gap in the rampart, with a seat to the right and an **OS trig point** away to the left, and walk down through the hillfort to return to the junction of paths. Go right here, then left on a narrow path below another limestone cliff before walking through a rock cutting to return to the ladder stile.

Retrace the outward route to the woodland edge, this time going slightly left along the field boundary to reach **King Arthur's Cave.** ◀ Keep to the left of the cave, walking along a lane below cliffs riddled with yet more cavities and passing the foundations of a limestone crusher for the nearby quarry, to return to the tarmac road just around the corner from the start of the walk at the entrance to **White Rocks Nature Reserve**.

The dramatic cave, which has a double entrance and two main chambers, provided a refuge for mammoths, hyenas, rhinoceros and cave lions in prehistoric times, and was occupied by man in the Palaeolithic era.

Looking out from the main chamber of King Arthur's cave

WALK 8

Coppet Hill and Goodrich

Start/Finish	Goodrich Castle car park (SO 575 196)
Distance	12km (7½ miles)
Ascent	235m (770ft)
Time	3–5hrs
Map	Outdoor Leisure 14
Public transport	Service 34 between Ross-on-Wye and Monmouth runs through Goodrich every two hours
Parking	Large car park and visitor centre south of Goodrich Castle

This is an outstanding walk with unrivalled views of the Wye as it leaves the plains of south Herefordshire and enters the gorge that defines the lower river. Coppet Hill is an important nature reserve and a wonderful recreational resource, and there is a suitably impressive climax to the walk at Goodrich Castle.

From the **castle car park** go back to the main road through Goodrich and turn left onto the lane signposted to Welsh Bicknor, crossing high above the B4229 on the Dry Arch – a brownstone bridge built to connect Coppet

The village of Goodrich and the Herefordshire hills

Hill and more especially the local landowners, the Vaughans of Courtfield, with the village. There are superb

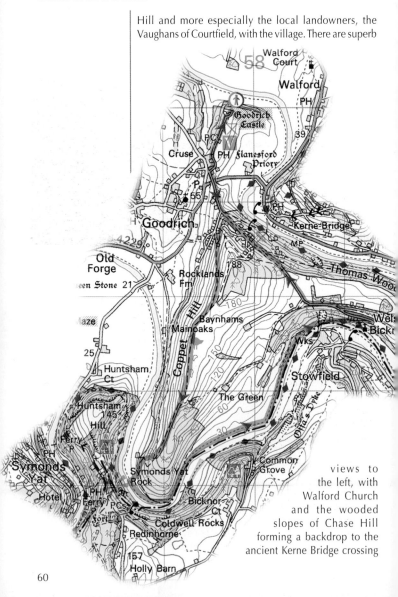

views to the left, with Walford Church and the wooded slopes of Chase Hill forming a backdrop to the ancient Kerne Bridge crossing

of the Wye, and then to the right, with Goodrich Church prominent on its ancient site.

Kerne Bridge and the flooded Wye from Coppet Hill

Just beyond Charlton (a 19th-century country house), the road divides. Take the steps rising steeply between the two branches, quickly reaching the pebbly quartz conglomerate outcrops (known as puddingstone) that underlie much of the ridge of **Coppet Hill**. The green path rises more gently now, running through woodland before emerging on the open hillside with the first of a series of sensational aerial views of the Wye floodplain as the river meanders round Huntsham Hill and approaches Symonds Yat.

The long ridge of **Coppet Hill** has outstanding views of the Wye Valley, the hills of south Herefordshire, Goodrich Castle and the wooded northern slopes of the Forest of Dean. More distantly, the Brecon Beacons, Clee Hills and the Malverns can all be seen. Much of the hill is a nature reserve, with fallow deer, nesting birds including yellowhammer

The 18th-century boundary wall next to the path on Coppet Hill

and linnet, butterflies such as the large skipper and green hairstreak, adders and grass snakes, and a ground plantlife that includes several species of orchids and autumn crocus on the limestone east of the summit ridge.

A very easy stroll leads to The Folly (constructed as a focal point in Courtfield's picturesque landscape and with an attached chapel but now a disappointingly insubstantial stone ruin) and then to one of the highlights of the walk: the long promenade on springy turf along the summit ridge. The path keeps just below the apex of the ridge, with thin woodland beyond a dilapidated wall to the left and the Wye far below to the right. ◄

Constructed from limestone quarried to the east of the ridge, the wall dates from the late 18th century and marked the boundary between the parishes of Goodrich and Welsh Bicknor.

Some distance beyond the end of the wood a gate leads into a field on the left and another fine view, this time down to the east. A little further to the south the ridge path passes the scanty remains of Jelemy Tump – a deserted hamlet named after an 18th-century squatter but last inhabited in the 1970s. The path now re-enters coppice woodland, still following the tumbledown wall and now descending quite gently but on slippery leaf litter to reach a stile giving access to a riverside meadow, with the Wye flowing left to right in front of the striking limestone cliffs of Coldwell Rocks. ▶

Turn left at the stile, picking up a riverside path (which can be submerged after winter rains) and passing a monument commemorating a tragedy when a child was swept away while swimming in the river. The path emerges from woodland and traverses a series of fields below **The Green**, with the Wye Valley Walk on an old railway line on the far bank. Somewhat incongruously, the derelict Edison Swan cable works (a crucial supplier of telephone cables in two world wars) appears across the river, which is then crossed by a bridge carrying the disused railway. It is worth climbing up onto the old bridge (now a footpath) to see the retrospective view down the Wye, with the conical hill of Rosemary Topping now very prominent to the left of the river.

Climb back down from the bridge, noting the entrance to the 600m-long Coppet Hill tunnel straight ahead and, slightly to the right, the concrete Second World War pillbox that defended the railway bridge. Continue along the riverbank for another 200m before

Since the 1970s, the rocks have achieved fame as a nesting site for peregrine falcons; the RSPB's observation point at Yat Rock, equipped with telescopes, can be seen to the right of the cliffs.

The riverside church at Welsh Bicknor

63

taking a left fork to reach the two buildings at the heart of **Welsh Bicknor** – the austere youth hostel, once a rectory, and the flamboyant High Victorian Church.

There is a choice of routes here: a lane to the left of the youth hostel zigzags up onto the plateau, while a path just west of the hostel climbs steeply up on steps then slants up to meet the lane (the path is more direct but is poorly signposted and was blocked by a massive fallen tree when last walked). The access lane to the former manor house at Courtfield soon comes in from the right. ◄ Keep straight on here to return to Goodrich, walking through attractive parkland on the plateau and then descending easily through woodland, passing a limestone quarry that supplied limekilns higher on the hill, and then walking past the puddingstone outcrops of Coppet Hill Nature Reserve.

Keep straight on along the lane, with another aerial view of Kerne Bridge and the refectory of the Augustinians' Flanesford Priory, to pick up the outward route by the steep steps and go over the Dry Arch to the Goodrich Castle access road. Turn right here to return to the **castle car park** and, more importantly, the castle itself, which forms a fitting climax to a superb walk.

The present red sandstone **castle**, magnificently sited on a spur above the river, dates largely from the 13th century and is well worth exploring, with an imposing barbican, a deep wide moat cut into the rock itself, a gatehouse with attached chapel, a tiny Norman keep and the substantial remains of the curtain wall with four corner towers.

Courtfield was the ancestral home of the Vaughan family, the boyhood home of the future Henry V and more recently a retreat house run by the Mill Hill Missionaries.

THE MIDDLE WYE
Ross-on-Wye to Hay-on-Wye

The descent to Aconbury, with Dinedor Hill in the background (Walk 12)

WALK 9

Sellack and Hoarwithy

Start/Finish	Hoarwithy Church (SO 545 294)
Distance	8km (5 miles)
Ascent	105m (345ft)
Time	2–3hrs
Map	Explorer 189
Public transport	Hoarwithy has four buses a day on service 44 between Ross-on-Wye and Hereford
Parking	Limited roadside parking in Hoarwithy

This is a walk through classic English lowland scenery, starting with a remarkable, highly ornate and richly decorated Italianate church in the attractive riverside village of Hoarwithy, passing two more churches and negotiating a Victorian suspension footbridge over the Wye.

Drop downhill from **Hoarwithy Church** to the village street, passing the Old Mill – a corn mill still in use in the 1970s – and taking the lane leading down to

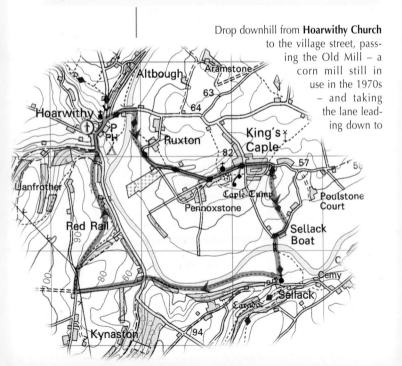

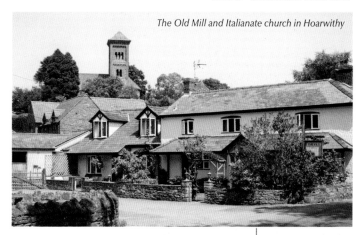

The Old Mill and Italianate church in Hoarwithy

Hoarwithy Bridge, with the strikingly tall former toll-house on the right just before the river crossing. ▶

The tollhouse was built when the first timber bridge was constructed in 1856 to replace the ancient ford and horse ferry across the river.

The **Church of St Catherine** at Hoarwithy was constructed in the 1880s in a Romanesque style, with a campanile and a cloister walk along the south side. The east end of the church has marble columns with large Byzantine capitals, and there are mosaic pavements too. Sadly the soft sandstone used in its construction has weathered badly and has repeatedly needed restoration.

Pause to savour the view back past the tollhouse to the church, then turn right on a wide green track just after crossing the bridge, keeping close to the riverbank, with waterfowl in the river and grey partridge on the track itself. Keep straight ahead when a lane comes in from the left, now with polytunnels on the left in season and a good view of King's Caple Church almost straight ahead.

The lane swings round to the left, now aligned with the course of a road (Caple Street) that is alleged to date back at least to Roman times, and which certainly drops down past Pennoxstone Court (a farmhouse expanded

67

into a large villa with park, pleasure grounds and walled garden) to an old ford on the Wye at Red Rail. **King's Caple Church** is now immediately on the left, with the low motte known as **Caple Tump** to the right. ◄

The steep-sided, circular motte was surrounded by a ditch and may once have had a castle keep on top, while the church, which has Jacobean box pews and pulpit, is situated in the former castle bailey.

Keep ahead on the lane running through the little village, passing the imposing 18th-century brick King's Caple Court (and, at a crossroads, the tiny Sunday and day school, built by subscription in 1840). Just beyond the modern school, take a hard-surface lane on the right for a few metres, then opt for the right-hand of two tracks, enclosed between tall hedges. Go through two metal gates, keep to the left-hand field margin and climb over a stile to cross an enormous arable field, with the path very obvious as it heads straight for a wooden stile in the distance. Beyond the stile the way lies to the right along a minor lane to **Sellack Boat**. On the right is the sculpture garden (open on summer Sundays) of Shieldbrook, which was once an inn called the Old Boar catering for bargees on the river. A rough track on the left here leads directly to the attractive suspension **footbridge** spanning the Wye.

The **bridge** at Sellack Boat dates from 1895, having been commissioned by Sellack's vicar to replace a ferry after recalcitrant boatmen had repeatedly refused to row him and other parishioners across the river – indeed, one vicar had previously used stilts to cross the river to avoid this problem! The bridge, with tubular cast iron pylons, is the best surviving example from the celebrated Louis Harper foundry.

The Wye by the suspension footbridge at Sellack Boat

Cross Sellack Common, site of a country fair, to reach **Sellack Church** – the only English church dedicated to St Tysilio and with a curious mix of medieval and Victorian work, together with the crumbling base of a medieval churchyard cross. The churches at Sellack, Hentland and King's Caple still observe the rare custom of distributing cakes after the Palm Sunday service. ▶ Take the path running west from the church, crossing the water meadows below Castlemeadow Wood, with the Jacobean mansion of Caradoc Court (restored after a devastating fire in 1986) out of sight on top of the ridge.

These pax cakes, handed out with the blessing 'peace and good neighbourhood', originated with a bequest from the then vicar, Thomas More, who died in 1448.

The river cliff to the west is impressive in places, with substantial exposures of Old Red Sandstone hinting at the erosive power of the river when its course lay on this side of the valley. Gradually the path nears the river, with mute swans plentiful at times, before curving left on a track that reaches the Hoarwithy road at Sheppon Hill stables. Go straight across, climbing up a lane that swings left to pass Hentland House (once the coach house of nearby Kynaston Court). Turn right before the house on a dusty track, then quickly fork right below a huge pylon onto a green and partly sunken track. Cross a stile, with the path down to the old ford at **Red Rail** going off to the right. ▶

The route lies straight on, eventually crossing a farm track, with superb views from this ridge-top vantage point of much of the country already walked, including the church spires at King's Caple and Sellack and, less pleasingly, the soft fruit polytunnels which are now a necessary evil in this part of Herefordshire. To the left of the path lies the ash plantation of Grandoo's Coppice (part of the Duchy of Cornwall's extensive Harewood End estate), and a little further on the route passes close to the farm at Llanfrother, which is the former site of a sixth-century monastic college and medieval hamlet whose earthworks can still be traced. One final stile takes the path through a copse and past some isolated cottages, then the way lies steeply down on a good woodland path to join the road through **Hoarwithy** just to the south of the excellent New Harp Inn.

Red Rail ford is recorded in 1652 but it lies on the route of the minor Roman road from King's Caple and excavations have proved the existence of a cobbled road. The route was stopped up after Hoarwithy Bridge was opened.

WALK 10

Capler Camp from Fownhope

Start/Finish	Fownhope recreation ground (SO 578 341)
Distance	10km (6 miles)
Ascent	315m (1035ft)
Time	3–4hrs
Map	Explorer 189
Public transport	Fownhope has seven buses a day on routes 453 and 454 from Hereford
Parking	Ample parking alongside the recreation field

This walk explores the country between the hills of the Woolhope Dome and the river plain of the Wye, visiting two iconic nature reserves on the way to a spectacular Iron Age hillfort and returning via the site of one of the many ferries across the Wye.

From the recreation field on the south-western edge of the large village and former river port of **Fownhope**, take the lane heading past the church, with the former village stocks to the right of the lych gate, cross the main road into Common Hill Lane and turn left into Church Croft to find a pleasant grassy path leading up between housing on the left and open countryside on the right. Curve right along the edge of the Nover Wood estate, then either climb up to the left to find and turn right along the Wye Valley Walk or (better still) descend to the right on a lower path, later a track, which rejoins Common Hill Lane by a wildflower bank, which is alive with the distinctive marbled white butterfly in high summer.

The lower route now turns left, uphill, past the village pump to reach the Wye Valley Walk at a complex junction. Go just to the left of a five-barred gate, with the entrance to Common Hill Nature Reserve and its wildflower meadow immediately on the left. The northward views of Haugh Wood and the intimate Woolhope Dome landscape are excellent. The path is easy to follow between orchards and scrubby hill slopes, then it climbs to

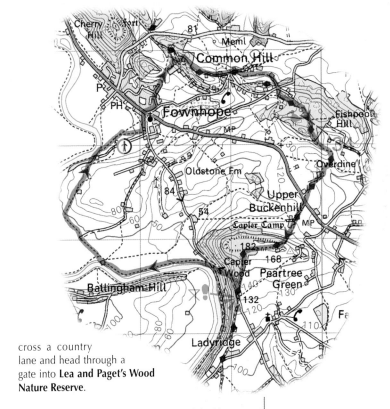

cross a country lane and head through a gate into **Lea and Paget's Wood Nature Reserve**.

One of the finest ancient, semi-natural deciduous woodlands in the whole of the Wye Valley, **Lea and Paget's Wood** is dominated by sessile oak and ash, and has superb drifts of bluebells in spring, with early purple and greater butterfly orchids later in the year. All three British woodpecker species are found, together with a breeding population of pied flycatchers and a number of butterflies, including white admirals and silver-washed fritillaries.

The very clear and well-shaded path passes a 19th-century limekiln on the left, and then winds through the woods to arrive at a welcome bench by an excellent viewpoint at the far end of the woodland. The path now

The view from south of Paget's Wood into the Woolhope Dome

follows the crest of a narrow ridge with wonderful countryside on both sides – Capler Camp, Aconbury Hill and the Wye Valley to the right, and the complicated ridges and valleys of the Woolhope Dome to the left.

The route descends into a little valley, crossing a stream and going around the left-hand side of a field below **Overdine Farm**, then goes straight ahead to reach the B4224 at Hill Crest. Go left here, then right in 100m along the Caplor Farm access track. On reaching the first of the farm buildings, turn left and then quickly right over a stile to climb through trees, along the right-hand side of an arable field and steeply on rustic steps through woodland to emerge by a barn at the edge of the impressive **Capler Camp hillfort**.

> The Iron Age **hillfort** at Capler Camp has a spectacular double rampart and ditches that are at places cut into the rock, and encloses a massive oval area of level ground. The camp is well known for its exceptional display of bluebells in May and the variety of woodland birds that can be seen. Fallow deer inhabit the woodland, which is dominated by oak, ash and lime.

Turn right here to walk through the fort or keep on the main path, which runs in the ditch around the south side of the ramparts before turning left on a shady path through woodland to descend to the famous viewpoint (sadly now largely obscured by trees) over the river Wye at Capler Lodge.

Take the road northwards from Capler Lodge, descending a steep hill until, just before the woodland ends on the left, taking the signposted footpath and, after just a few metres, turning right to drop down on a narrow path to the riverbank. Turn right again and follow the tranquil river upstream, crossing a footbridge and then a potato field, with the old ferryman's cottage at Mancell's Ferry in view ahead. Just before the cottage it is possible to scramble down to inspect the site of the ferry crossing, which is still very clear at low water. ▶

The ferry operated until the early 20th century, latterly by Samuel Terry, who was the parish clerk at Ballingham on the west side of the river.

Go over a stile into the garden of the ferryman's cottage, skirting round to reach the field beyond. A path continues alongside the river, but the path off to the right, visible as a clear crop mark heading for a metal gate on the far side of the field, offers a more attractive return to Fownhope. Cross a second, much narrower, field to a

The site of Mancell's Ferry – the old river crossing from Fownhope to Ballingham

Looking west across the Wye from near Leabrink

wooden gate and footbridge, then go slightly right across a track and follow the right-hand hedge of a huge meadow, walking just above the edge of the floodplain. Go through the gate on the right at the end of the field (a waymark disc is helpful here) and climb gently, veering left to follow a faint track towards a field barn. A gate beyond this gives access to the top of a long pasture; go straight ahead both here and in the next field, on a thin path through crops, now with an excellent prospect across the river to the gently rising fields around Holme Lacy.

Bear half-right across a meadow and then down a little ramp to a gate giving access to the garden of the attractive riverside house (formerly a pair of cottages) at Leabrink. Go straight ahead, passing a couple of riverside benches and taking the right-hand of two paths, leaving the river to return to the recreation field at **Fownhope**.

WALK 11
Haugh Wood

Start/Finish	Forestry Commission car park at Haugh Wood (SO 592 365)
Distance	8km (5 miles)
Ascent	190m (620ft)
Time	3hrs
Map	Explorer 189
Public transport	None
Parking	Forestry Commission car park on the minor road from Mordiford to Woolhope

This intricate but easy walk explores the highest land of the Woolhope Dome – an area of Llandovery sandstone rising above hills and hidden valleys east of the Wye. The superb wildflowers of Joan's Hill and the nationally important butterflies of Haugh Wood are at their best in late spring or early summer.

Start at the left-hand corner of the car park, passing Forestry Commission and butterfly trail information boards and going north on a good gravel track with a thin belt of deciduous woodland on each side and darker conifer stands behind. ▶ Go straight across at a walkers' crossroads, now on a greener track that curves right and descends between brambles and bracken to a T-junction. Turn left, on gravel again and with a metal gate coming into view ahead. Climb the stile next to the gate to enter Joan's Hill Farm Nature Reserve.

Now under the astute stewardship of the charity Plantlife, this **nature reserve** is an amazing oasis of unchanging small pasture fields with a fine out-look towards the Wye Valley. The 19ha (46-acre) site contains small fields and orchards enclosed by wide hedgerows, and includes a number of unim-proved old hay meadows boasting classic wildflow-ers such as green-winged orchid in May and lady's

Mixed woodland is characteristic of Haugh Wood, which was once managed as broadleaved coppice but was then converted to conifer forest in the 1960s by the Forestry Commission; it is now being managed more sympathetically again.

Joan's Hill Farm Nature Reserve with Backbury Hill beyond

bedstraw in June. The cider apple orchard dates back to the 1840s and includes classic varieties such as foxwhelp and Herefordshire redstreak.

The view ahead is superb, across the reserve to the wooded slopes of Backbury Hill, but the way lies down-hill, along a track following the right-hand edge of the field, which is awash with cowslips and common spotted orchids in early summer. Negotiate a muddy area at the bottom of the slope and ignore a field opening on the right, with a view of the scattered settlement of Checkley beyond a damp pasture, and instead climb on the footpath to enter a cider apple orchard, its trees festooned with mistletoe, with Joan's Hill farmhouse immediately behind.

In 1811, this seemingly innocuous little stream caused disaster when, following a severe storm, the swollen brook swept away a barn, a cottage and a cider mill, claiming four lives in the process.

To continue on the main route turn left at the metal gate at the far end of the orchard, but to extend the walk go through the gate and then steeply downhill to the right, passing through Limburies Wood and swinging left on a good track that descends to a bridge crossing the Pentaloe Brook. ◄ Just before the bridge is the site of a medieval **moated homestead** with a pond alongside, although the remains are hidden in scrubby woodland

and it takes good archaeological knowledge or a vivid imagination to reconstruct the layout. Climb back up the track to return to the orchard.

Leave the orchard through a gateway to the right and keep to the left of a tall hedge, now with knapweed to the left in July and Joan's Hill farmhouse well seen to the right. ▶ Swing slightly left through another open field gateway, following the right-hand edge of a field to enter woodland over a stile in the far corner. Swing immediately left on a good path, then left again after 300m to reach a forest road just inside the northern boundary of **Haugh Wood**. Turn right here, then right again after only a few metres, following the gravelly track straight on at a crossroads until the public road is reached at Haughwoods.

The 17th-century timber-framed farmhouse is a classic example of Herefordian black-and-white architecture and, together with its stone outbuildings, it makes an attractive composition in its wooded surroundings.

Occupying the highest land in the Woolhope Dome, **Haugh Wood** is an ancient woodland that was owned in medieval times by Hereford Cathedral, but which was later bought by the Forestry Commission, who described it in the 1960s as 'grossly unproductive'. Much is now conifer plantation, but the broad-leaved fringes and forest rides are hugely important for invertebrates, and the wood is also home to fallow deer, badgers, dormice and polecats, together with sparrowhawks and tawny owls.

Continue straight ahead across the road, quickly branching left and then ignoring paths and forest roads to the left and right until the Forestry Commission's butterfly trail is picked up at a complex

One of the butterfly rides in Haugh Wood

Haugh Wood is nationally important for its collection of woodland butterflies, many of which are rare in the UK. White letter hairstreak, high brown fritillary, pearl-bordered fritillary and wood whites are among the star attractions.

junction of tracks and footpaths. ◄ The key now is to follow the green waymark posts, which make route-finding straightforward as the trail winds through the southern part of the wood, merging with a forest road and then swinging left to approach the boundary of the wood (look out for white admirals here).

Keep left again, using a series of forest rides that act as wildlife corridors, with cleared areas at the side of the tracks that have been colonised by brambles and other specialist food and nectar plants, thus attracting specific butterflies. At regular intervals there are information panels explaining the butterflies that might be present, especially on sunny and warm afternoons. A left turn back into the woodland, with a good possibility of seeing marbled whites, and a sharper left turn onto a footpath are both indicated by green waymark posts, as is the final right turn leading back to the car park.

WALK 12
Aconbury Hill

Start/Finish	Little Birch village hall (SO 505 324)
Distance	11km (7 miles)
Ascent	260m (855ft)
Time	3–4hrs
Map	Explorer 189
Public transport	Bus services 32 and 33 between Hereford and Ross-on-Wye offer an hourly service to King's Thorn (1km or ½ mile west of Little Birch village hall)
Parking	Limited parking by the village hall (honesty box)

This is an easy but exhilarating walk with sensational views north to Hereford Cathedral from the fort on the summit of Aconbury Hill, and more intimate views along quiet green lanes and through woodlands carpeted with spring flowers.

Take a look at the Primitive Methodist chapel (now sadly disused) just along the road from the village hall at **Little Birch**, and follow the green lane just to its right, passing a water pump and stone trough. Turn right at an information board to enter the Aconbury woodlands, using a clear track that rises almost imperceptibly through mature trees – which have been vigorously thinned and which support an impressive array of birdlife, including jays and both green and great spotted woodpeckers. Keep straight on when paths leave on either side, to arrive surprisingly quickly at the southern ramparts of the **Aconbury Hill hillfort**.

> The Iron Age **hillfort** on the summit of Aconbury Hill is massive, enclosing 7ha (17 acres) within an impressive earthen rampart and ditch. Even now the earth bank rises to 5m (16ft) in places. The fort was occupied from the second century BC until after the collapse of the Roman Empire some 600 years later, and was then reused as a vantage point by Parliamentarian forces during the English Civil War.

Fork right at a waymark post inside the fort, going past the **trig point** to inspect the wide views towards Hereford from the northern ramparts, then retrace your steps to follow a path running the length of the fort, awash with bluebells in season. Ignore all diverging paths and eventually go through the western bank and ditch with the help of guide rails to descend gently on a path running between young conifers to the left and oak, beech and sweet chestnut to the right. Follow a yellow waymarked track through coppiced woodland, then turn right on a forest road, now with a good view north beyond Mount Skippitt to the Hereford plain.

The forest road gradually curves east, just inside the woodland edge, eventually rising to a viewpoint with an excellent prospect north and east, over Dinedor Hill and the Woolhope Dome. Ignore the footpath carrying the Violette Szabo trail – which commemorates the life of a wartime heroine, and ends at a museum in nearby Wormelow – but when the trees reappear on the left take a path dropping steeply down through the woodland to emerge in a large arable field.

Looking north from Aconbury Hill to Hereford and Dinedor Hill

Aim for the right-hand line of trees and follow a stream down to the right, with **St Ann's Well** hidden in the little tree-lined valley to the left. ▶ Cross the stream just above a pond to reach the narrow lane on the edge of the hamlet of Aconbury. The route takes the path heading over a stile to the right just before **Aconbury Court**, but it is worth pressing on for a few metres to inspect Aconbury Church, now long disused.

St Ann's Well rises in a stone pool with medieval origins. Its waters are reputed to be especially beneficial for the eye, especially if taken on Twelfth Night.

The present **Aconbury Court** is the successor of a mansion house with walled gardens built in the 16th century on the site of an Augustinian nunnery founded 300 years earlier. The church has blocked doorways that once offered access from the cloisters of the nunnery to the nave and chancel of the church, and several brackets for roof timbers where the upper floor of the claustral buildings bordered the church.

Back on the footpath, drop down to cross a marshy area between two fishponds and swing right on a footpath skirting another large arable field above the higher fishpond, where tufted duck and Canada geese can sometimes be seen. A stile leads into Guy's Wood, its name a reminder that the land was once owned by Guy's Hospital. Keep to the left-hand edge of the wood, then strike up a clear path through **Wallbrook Wood**, finally

Wood anemones carpeting the floor of Athelstans Wood

This woodland, with its wild garlic and bluebells, was owned by the Bishops of Hereford from Saxon times until the dissolution.

The present building was paid for by its vicar, Stephen Thackwell, in 1869, and includes a polygonal apse and a wrought iron screen.

swinging left to reach and cross a country lane. Go slightly to the right across a meadow, with the extensive buildings of **Merrivale Farm**, an organic dairy enterprise, coming into view to the left.

Cross the farm's access track via two awkward stiles and make for a stile in the far left corner of a second field. Turn right along a track following an ancient holloway up to Green Farm, then left through a gate, now on a superb green lane that passes a couple of oaks with massive trunks and crosses a lane to enter **Athelstans Wood**. ◄ Turn right again on reaching a wider track, now following Herefordshire Trail waymarks as the path leaves the wood to cross a field, then re-enter the trees, going through coppiced woodland with a stunning carpet of wood anemones in April. Drop down on a very clear path to cross the Wriggles Brook on a curious earthen bridge.

Climb the hillside opposite to reach a narrow lane in the hamlet of Skyrme, turning right to pass St Mary's Church in its elevated churchyard. ◄ From the graveyard there is a good view down into the yard of Church Farm, with its old cider press and assorted antique agricultural

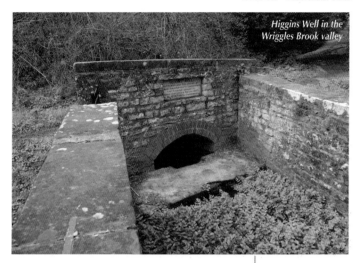

Higgins Well in the Wriggles Brook valley

implements. Just beyond the church take the rough track on the right, which quickly descends into the Wriggles Brook valley again, with Higgins Well in view ahead. ▸

Go past the well to climb a muddy lane (big boulders are a help here) and pass attractive cottages to reach a quiet road. Turn right, then keep straight on between fields with wild daffodils, eventually taking a green path uphill to a crossroads with the Castle Inn – which has suffered a series of closures in recent years – just on the right. Take the lane straight ahead but after 300m veer right onto a footpath that swings left over a stile and then runs between tall hedges to reach the road through **Little Birch**, with the village hall just to the right.

The structure dates from the early 19th century and was restored in 1897 to commemorate Queen Victoria's Diamond Jubilee

WALK 13

Breinton Springs

Start/Finish	High Town, Hereford (SO 510 400)
Distance	12km (7½ miles)
Ascent	50m (165ft)
Time	3–4hrs
Map	Explorer 189
Public transport	Hereford has regular train connections from Manchester, Cardiff, Worcester and London
Parking	Car parks (fee payable) and some on-street parking in Hereford

Hereford Cathedral provides a unifying theme for this gentle walk, with the great building itself dominating the early stages and the ruined country house of medieval cathedral treasurers a surprising discovery in the quiet apple orchard village of Breinton.

The Norman cathedral, with its chained library and Mappa Mundi museum, is well worth a visit.

Take the alley in the south-west corner of High Town (still the site of an outdoor market on Wednesdays) to follow the pedestrianised Church Street into Cathedral Close. ◀ Skirt around the right-hand side of **Hereford Cathedral** and then cross the ancient Wye Bridge – constructed in 1490 to replace an earlier wooden bridge – before turning right on a combined cycle and footpath, which hugs the river as far as Hunderton Bridge. Climb a flight of steps to cross the Wye on the bridge, which carried the Barton station branch of the Newport, Abergavenny and Hereford Railway, then drop down to take a path on the north bank past a cricket field.

Rarely open but unexpectedly fascinating, this museum (housed in the city's Victorian water pumping station) traces the history of drinking water provision and has a number of steam engines.

A short diversion along a lane to the right leads past the Broomy Hill miniature railway to Hereford's **waterworks museum**. ◀ The main route continues to follow the river upstream on a grassy path that is alive with small tortoiseshell butterflies in summer. The wooded riverbank provides habitat for birds such as

The 15th-century Wye Bridge in the centre of Hereford

long-tailed tits, chiffchaffs and willow warblers, while on the river itself there are large numbers of mute swans together with Canada geese and the occasional goosander.

The path arrives abruptly at a riverside meadow and then climbs briefly up a red earth path, with Breinton Springs down to the left. ▶ Turn right just before reaching a little car park to explore the orchard around **St Michael's Church**, heavily restored in the

A freshwater spring still flows here at the side of a 'cliff' close to the river.

1860s. To the north of the church is the site of a deserted medieval village, while to the south a ringwork is all that remains of Breinton Camp.

> Built around 1150 and abandoned by the end of the 13th century, the moated **Breinton Camp** was the country house of the treasurer of Hereford Cathedral. The site now consists of a low mound surrounded by a dry moat, with little evidence above ground of the once extensive residence. A holloway immediately to the west led to a ford across the Wye, which was extensively used by drovers.

Go back to the car park and follow the lane past Breinton House – a Georgian house whose gardens were described as 'exceedingly picturesque' in 1916, when there were tennis and croquet lawns, a kitchen garden, orchards and riverside walks. Turn left at the end of the lane, passing through the little hamlet of **Lower Breinton**, then head to the right through a copse and along the right-hand edge of arable and pasture fields, with improving views westwards to the long ridge of the Black Mountains.

Cross a minor road and continue straight ahead across three more fields, with yellowhammers and whitethroats overhead and orchards (the cider and dessert apple blossom especially attractive here) on the left, to reach Green Lane, once part of a droving route from Mid Wales to Hereford and London. Turn right here onto the old drove route, initially a narrow path with Wyevale Wood Nature Reserve to the left. ◀ Later the drove road becomes a gravelly track running past isolated cottages, and then past King's Acre – where Drovers Pond provided drinking water for the animals being driven to market – and on to a staggered crossroads of bridleways, with Drovers Wood (planted as recently as 2001 on former arable land) ahead on the left.

Turn south at the crossroads, passing the half-timbered Upper Hill Farm, which once boasted its own cider mill and still retains a 17th-century weatherboarded

Consisting of secondary woodland on an ancient woodland site, Wyevale Wood is home to nuthatches and great spotted woodpeckers.

threshing barn. Turn left along a quiet country lane, passing an old cider press at the entrance to Little Breinton Farm, then take the even quieter lane on the right, now with the tower of Belmont Abbey ahead and Aconbury Hill in the distance to its left. The lane zigzags left and then right, goes slightly right across a road near **Warham Farm**, and curves sharply left: take the signposted fisherman's path to the right here, passing below the imposing Warham House. ▶

The fisherman's path descends almost imperceptibly through meadows to reach the riverside footpath. Turn left here and reverse the outward route alongside the river past the **waterworks museum** and across Hunderton Bridge to reach the Wye Bridge, **Hereford Cathedral** and the great market place of High Town.

Hereford Cathedral from River Walk

Rebuilt in 1854 in Jacobean style, the existing Warham House replaced an earlier house on the same site. It stands in landscaped parkland, with a series of little pools in a valley.

WALK 14

Black and White Weobley

Start/Finish	Weobley Church (SO 401 518)
Distance	7km (4½ miles)
Ascent	105m (345ft)
Time	2–3hrs
Maps	Explorer 201, 202
Public transport	Bus 461 runs between Hereford and Llandrindod Wells every hour, calling at Broad Street in Weobley
Parking	Village car park in Bell Square

This is an easy stroll in typically lush Herefordshire countryside below the cornstone ridge of the Wormsley Hills. Weobley was a medieval borough with a Thursday market and once sent two MPs to Westminster. It still has an urban feel, with black-and-white houses lining the main streets.

Broad Street and the church of St Peter & St Paul, Weobley

Start at Weobley's prominent **church**, with Norman doorway, a magnificent spire and sandstone preaching cross on lichen-encrusted 14th-century steps in the churchyard,

before heading past the classically half-timbered Red Lion, with a cruck-framed medieval hall house behind, into the centre of the village. Climb Broad Street, pausing to take in the sight of so many unusually early (14th- and 15th-century) black-and-white buildings, and carry straight on at the top of the street into a lane running between houses and past a red telephone box into the **castle grounds**.

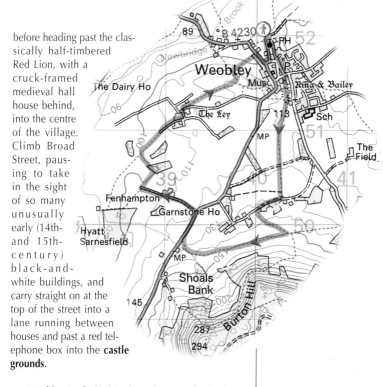

Weobley Castle, built in the 11th century by the de Lacy family – a noble French family that took part in the Norman Conquest – once had solid stone battlements with round corner towers. When the antiquarian John Leland visited in 1535 he described is as 'a goodly castell, but somewhat in decay'. All that is left now are grassy banks and a deep double ditch.

Take the path going straight ahead past the remains of the motte and the deep southern ditch, with the site of a medieval mill down to the right. Go through a gate and bear slightly right, heading for another field gate that gives access to a rough lane running just inside the right-hand side of a field, with the scarp slope of the cornstone ridge straight ahead. Keep straight on across a stony track, go through a kissing gate and quickly turn right in front of a gate with barbed wire and warnings about private property. The route is now following the inner boundary of the Garnstone Park estate, although the few remaining buildings give few clues to its former status.

> **Garnstone Castle** was designed by renowned British architect John Nash in 1807, replacing an earlier house. A castellated mansion, it was one of the last (and worst) of Nash's designs, and it was demolished in the 1950s. Little of the fabric remains, although the parkland still has avenues of Wellingtonias. There are traces of the walled garden and, higher up the hill, the extensive deer park.

Go across a stile into a rough lane, but at a waymark turn left at a kissing gate to enter a big arable field. The route lies diagonally to the left, aiming for another kissing gate in the distance: it can be hard going after the field has been ploughed. It is worth going through the gate and briefly along the lane to get a distant glimpse

Looking back along the path that descends from the slopes of Burton Hill

of the entrance gates to the former mansion and an adjacent ha-ha, and the oddly named Snuff Box Pool a little further to the east, but the main walk turns sharply back to the west to cross the arable field again, on a level course below the steep fields and woodlands of **Burton Hill**, going to the left of a lone tree to reach a gap in the hedgerow and a useful waymark post.

Keep on across another arable field, with a fine view north-west across the forlorn remains of Fields End Farm, with cider house, stables and dairy alongside, and find a gate giving access onto a green lane. Go straight across two more fields – the hedgerows here are thick with pheasants, while buzzards and red kites swoop overhead, and stubble is left to encourage lapwings to breed – cross a track and take the obvious path through a final field to reach the B4230. Turn right along the road, then left after 400m along the Fenhampton Farm access road, with the site of a deserted medieval village over the hedge to the right. ▶

Stay on the track past **Fenhampton**, with a glimpse of Hay Bluff and the long ridge of the Black Mountains to the left, and then take a permissive path on the right just after a hedge. This becomes a green track, curves left and then turns right across a footbridge and through a gate into a long, narrow field, now heading back towards Weobley. The path becomes a drive, which is well signposted as it goes to the left of substantial farm buildings. Go past a decorative cider press and an oast house to arrive suddenly at the extraordinary sight of **The Ley**. ▶

The way now lies over a stile into a paddock and then through two gates to follow the right-hand edge of a field. Walk across a potato field, with Weobley Church now dominating the scene ahead, and around a final field to find a sunken green lane that quickly arrives at the road through **Weobley**. Turn right here to follow the road back to the car park and **church**.

Fenhampton is a classic Jacobean gabled farmhouse in the Herefordian black-and-white style with painted brick and rendered infill.

Built in 1589, the half-timbered Grade I listed house features an impressive set of eight gabled roofs, windows and porch.

WALK 15

Arthur's Stone and Merbach Common

Start/Finish	Bredwardine Bridge (SO 336 446)
Distance	11km (7 miles)
Ascent	290m (950ft)
Time	3–4hrs
Map	Outdoor Leisure 13
Public transport	Bredwardine has no public transport services useful for walkers
Parking	Informal parking for a few cars near the bridge

This is a magnificent walk with one strenuous climb, compensated for by terrific views into the Golden Valley from the Neolithic tomb of Arthur's Stone and in all directions from the modest summit of Merbach Hill. The medieval parkland landscape around Bredwardine Church is an added bonus.

Take the path on the west bank downstream from the delightful

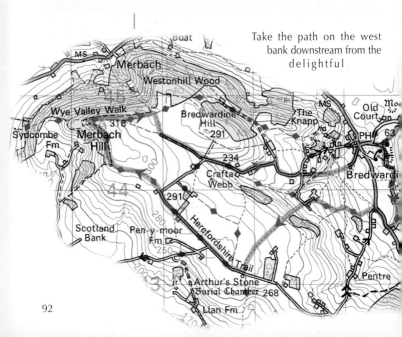

multi-arched 17th-century **bridge** over the River Wye, with a tollhouse close by, and climb through a meadow to **Bredwardine Church**. ▶ A bridleway runs between the church and the community orchard, then dips down with the overgrown mound of a late medieval castle on the left. A path to the left passes between the castle and some equally overgrown fishponds (part of a designed landscape that also included a kitchen garden, orchard and vineyard) to reach the bank of the Wye, but keep to the main path through woodland and to the right of the much more substantial water feature of Pond Bay – another medieval fishpond.

The church has a blocked-up Saxon doorway with eroded carvings above, including a sheela na gig, and was the last parish of the celebrated Victorian diarist Francis Kilvert, who is buried in the churchyard.

A path allegedly leaves to the right here but appears to have been lost, so keep ahead on the bridleway, going half-right through pasture and right along a track to reach the B4352. Go briefly right along the mercifully quiet main road, turn left onto the Dorstone road but after only 100m take the path on the right. This is initially overgrown but quickly improves as it crosses pasture. ▶ It is vital to turn right at the top of the field, to climb a grassy bank and reach a stile in the left corner of the next field, then cross sheep pastures to reach Finestreet Farm, which has some original 17th-century timber-framing.

A kissing gate straight ahead gives access to Wern Wood Nature Reserve, noted for its rookery, but the ground here is rough and wet.

Turn left along the farm's access road and go straight on, uphill, on a path heading directly towards the ridge ahead. The first field is quite steep and the second much more so, although the retrospective views across the Wye Valley become increasingly impressive as height is gained. The stile at the top of this field is tall, rickety and slopes downhill (unless the county council has responded to requests to fix it!) but once it has been conquered the slope eases, with the path crossing grassy pasture, a clover ley and a potato field before arriving suddenly and thrillingly at **Arthur's Stone** on the ridgetop.

The magnificent late Neolithic chambered tomb of **Arthur's Stone** is superbly situated on a narrow ridge above the Golden Valley, with a spectacular

The Neolithic chambered tomb of Arthur's Stone on Dorstone Hill

capstone six metres long weighing 25 tons. Nine upright stones remain, together with a right-angled entrance passage, all of which would have been covered by an earthen mound. Bizarrely, the monument is now fenced off, although the fence is utterly inadequate as a deterrent to visitors.

The common land of Merbach Hill is noted for skylarks and birds of prey, and has sensational views down to the meanders of the River Wye and out to the Malverns, Clee Hill, the Radnor Hills and the Black Mountains.

Head north-west along the narrow lane, a successor to the prehistoric trackway that connected a series of sites along the ridge. To the left is the upper Golden Valley – one of the unspoilt treasures of western Herefordshire – with the long ridge of the Black Mountains behind. The lane is long but virtually traffic-free, and when it swings right the way lies straight ahead through a gate. Follow the gravelly track until it swings away to the left, then keep to the right-hand side of the hedge, climbing very gradually and curving round to the right to find the gate leading on to **Merbach Hill**. ◄

A narrow green path crosses the left-hand edge of the common, with spectacular views down into and

across the Wye Valley, eventually reaching the bright white **trig pillar** marking the summit of the hill. Take the clear path going east, dropping down through woodland and then winding through bracken augmented by rosebay willowherb to reach the edge of the common at an information board. Turn right here, then left through a gate onto a very well-defined green lane, thick with hedgerow birds, which reaches a tarmac road just above **Crafta Webb**.

Impressive meander loops of the Wye from Merbach Hill

> While the easily visible remains of the deserted hamlet of **Crafta Webb** are disappointing, its history is extraordinary. It was a squatter settlement established in the early 19th century following a bequest of £30,000 from George Jarvis, a former tramp who became wealthy after emigrating to the US. The settlement grew rapidly and boasted its own grocer, tailor and shoemaker, but by the 1920s many of the cottages were deserted and now only a few crumbling foundations remain.

Bredwardine Bridge

Keep to the lane as it descends gently between grassland and newly planted orchards, often with wide views across the Wye, aiming for a green path descending from Fine Street back to Bredwardine. The view ahead is exceptional, with the red sandstone river-cliff of Bosbury Scar prominent, backed by the Woolhope Dome and the distant Malvern Hills. Over a stile the descent steepens, through a field with exceptional foxgloves and through a wooded dell, to emerge on a clear path heading directly towards Bredwardine Church. A final trek along a rutted track leads past the village hall and the Red Lion to the main road and, just beyond, the lane leading back to the village church and the **bridge**.

WALK 16
Kilvert's Clyro

Start/Finish	Hay-on-Wye Buttermarket (SO 229 424)
Distance	10km (6 miles)
Ascent	260m (855ft)
Time	3–4hrs
Map	Outdoor Leisure 13
Public transport	Bus 39 runs every two hours between Hereford and Brecon via Hay-on-Wye
Parking	Hay-on-Wye has a large car park on Oxford Road south of the town centre

Centred around the historic village of Clyro, where village life in the 1860s was brought to life in Francis Kilvert's diaries while he was curate there, this walk also explores the scenic banks of the Wye above Hay and climbs the valley slopes to discover hidden farms and sumptuous views.

From the 19th-century Buttermarket below the ruins of Hay Castle the walk takes narrow streets on the left to

Looking across the Wye to the Warren, a beauty spot near Hay-on-Wye

Wyecliff took its name from the steep river cliffs formed when the Wye cut through the thick glacial deposits that virtually blocked the valley here.

reach Broad Street and then crosses **Hay Bridge** on the B4351. The path is well signposted (as the Wye Valley Walk) as it leaves the road and runs around the right-hand side of an arable field, then skirts the stone boundary wall of **Wyecliff**, with great views down to the rapids as the Wye swings around a tight meander. ◄

The small border market town of **Hay-on-Wye**, lying just in Wales and boasting a Norman motte and later stone castle, rose from 20th-century obscurity at the hands of second-hand bookseller Richard Booth and now hosts an acclaimed literary festival every June. Its position at the junction of Offa's Dyke Path and the Wye Valley Walk ensures that it is also a major destination for walkers in the Welsh borders.

The path keeps close to the riverbank as it makes its way around an enormous arable field, with The Barn prominently in view to the right below the

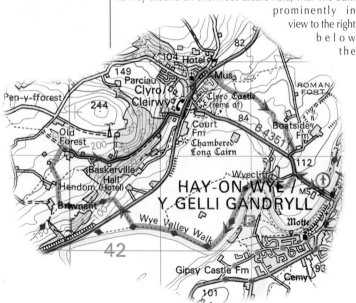

slopes of Forest Wood, while the Wye flows attractively to the left. The river here is picturesque in the extreme and is well-used, with a variety of canoes and small boats on the water and footpaths on both banks. Eventually the route leaves the riverbank, still following the **Wye Valley Walk** as it crosses the main road and climbs to the left across pasture, aiming for an obvious gap between two woods. The retrospective view of the valley and the Black Mountains behind is ample compensation for the effort involved in the climb.

Go through a gate and keep to the right-hand hedge line, but just before **Briwnant** turn right, leaving the Wye Valley Walk here and climbing towards **Hendom** – one of a number of late medieval encroachments onto the waste around here. The route is complex but obvious, going diagonally across one field to an awkward stile and then through a new gate to edge around the farm to the right. Immediately beyond the farm, bear half-left across an upland pasture to find a well-hidden stile on the right, then keep ahead to reach a somewhat rickety stile that provides access into Llowes Common. ▶

The existing Llowes Common, now dominated by bracken and scrubby birch, represents a valuable survival from a much bigger area that was largely enclosed in the 18th century.

Somewhat surprisingly the common is well-wooded, and the path meanders (through bluebells in spring) across a boggy area to cross two stiles and reach a quiet country lane. Turn right along this (a path on the left gives access to the attractive eastern segment of the common) and follow it down through Cwmsirhwy Wood and above the **Baskerville Hall Hotel** to the main road. ▶ Turn left along the pavement and quickly left again into the village of **Clyro**, passing the church on the left to reach the centre of the village.

Baskerville Hall was once a country house known as Clyro Court, where Sir Arthur Conan Doyle is believed to have stayed while writing *The Hound of the Baskervilles*.

The village of **Clyro** repays quiet exploration, with a tree-covered castle mound, a big rookery, a number of ancient cottages including Sacred Cottage – originally the priest's house – and plenty of Kilvert associations including a plaque in the church, the former vicarage, the school where he taught and Ashbrook House, his former home. At the south end of the village, Court Farm was once a grange farm

The northern scarp of the Black Mountains from the edge of Llowes Common

of Abbeycwmhir, and there is a megalithic chambered tomb in the field beyond the farm.

Just beyond the little stream by the Bridge Stores, turn right with Kilvert's house alongside. The track quickly reaches the main road again, with a path on the far side clearly signposted slightly to the left. Go across a dilapidated stile into a long narrow field, with the line of the path faint but clear and Clyro Mill – a corn mill that was worked until the 1920s – down to the left. Cross a stile to go round an arable field, cresting the ridge to be confronted by the forbidding scarp of the Black Mountains straight ahead and the Brecon Beacons to the right.

Rough pasture lies beyond a metal gate, with a thin path cutting across to a stile. On the left is Tir Mynach, which was once part of a monastic grange, with the former spring known as the Monks' Well alongside. Further to the east, near **Boatside Farm**, is the site of a short-lived Roman fort indicated by a rock-cut ditch and turf banks. Go half-right on a narrow path through the next field to a stile in the far corner, then follow the right-hand edge of a final field to another metal gate. The lane here leads back in about 100m to the main road, with a final left turn leading across the **bridge** back to Hay.

UPPER MIDDLE WYE
Hay-on-Wye to Newbridge-on-Wye

Park Wood and Radnor Forest from Rhos Fach Common (Walk 17)

WALK 17
Talgarth and Llanelieu

Start/Finish	Talgarth Mill (SO 154 336)
Distance	9km (6 miles)
Ascent	285m (935ft)
Time	3–4hrs
Map	Outdoor Leisure 13
Public transport	Talgarth has a bus roughly every two hours on service 39 from Hereford to Brecon
Parking	Free car park to the west of the town centre

A gentle walk through spectacular scenery in the Black Mountains foothills, visiting a superb isolated church and the Brecknock Wildlife Trust's most popular reserve, with woodland, waterfalls and abundant birdlife.

Park Wood, which has been owned by the Woodland Trust since 1985, consists of recent plantations on an ancient woodland site, with beech, oak and ash predominant.

Leave **Talgarth Mill** – an 18th-century corn mill (later a fulling mill, a dentist's and then a butcher's) that has been superbly restored and now has a bakery and café attached – by finding The Bank and then Church Street, aiming to the right of the church and then taking the track heading straight for Park Wood, going through a gate and then steadily uphill across three fields, with good retrospective views of the Brecon Beacons beyond the town of Talgarth, to find a stile giving access to the woodland. ◀ Climb steeply up steps just inside the woodland and zigzag left and right across a track, taking the waymarked path and gradually rising through beech woodland with occasional yews to arrive at a stile at the upper edge of the wood.

Turn left and contour around the edge of a large field, with a magnificent prospect across Cwm Rhyd-Ellywe of the long ridge of the Black Mountains, followed by a less magnificent march through high bracken in summer. Beyond the bracken the way lies along the crest of the ridge, passing through rough grazing and now with an equally extensive view to the left, looking across the fertile

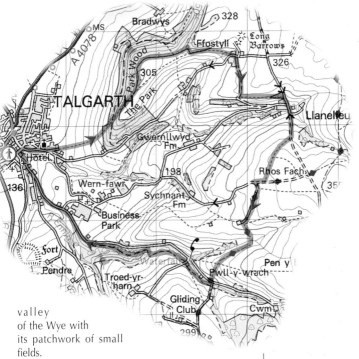

valley
of the Wye with
its patchwork of small
fields.

The route descends gently through
a series of fields to reach a narrow lane at **Ffostyll Farm**.
Two **long barrows** lie in a field to the left here (ask permission at the farm to view them). ▶ Take the path heading south from the farm, at first alongside a barn and then as a rough track across two fields, with a right-angled turn at the foot of the second field bringing the path down to another narrow lane just above the 17th-century **Llanelieu Court**, which has a niche and inscribed stone in the wall opposite. Turn downhill to find the flight of stone steps leading to the churchyard.

The ancient **Church of St Ellyw at Llanelieu** is remote, secluded and outwardly unexceptional, but the interior is remarkable, with the big red-painted rood screen separating nave from sanctuary a startling survival from the 14th century, and

The Neolithic chambered tombs have suffered damage over the centuries and are somewhat overgrown, but a number of stones are still upright and their situation at the foot of the mountains is impressive.

103

The 'hidden' church at Llanelieu

a collection of medieval and post-Reformation wall paintings including one depicting Adam and Eve, the serpent and the Tree of Life. Access is via an oversized key kept at Llanelieu Court.

Continue south along the little lane, passing the Whipping Tree – an old yew tree allegedly used as the village stocks – then rise steeply and cross a cattle grid before swinging right on a track that runs just inside the boundary of **Rhos Fach Common**, which was formerly used by the poor to graze pigs, sheep and cows and is now a valuable area of open moorland below the Black Mountain ridge, with the Brecon Beacons to the west and the rolling hills of Mid Wales beyond the Wye Valley to the north. Turn right on joining a road, with gliders soaring overhead during the summer, then quickly left onto a bridleway – actually a metalled lane – that runs between tall hedges down to Berth-fedw.

Go left just before the farm buildings, crossing a concrete yard to a gate to pick up a sunken lane, which drops increasingly steeply over slabs and loose boulders of the underlying Old Red Sandstone to ford a small stream. Continue on the track as it rises above the left bank of

the stream in its surprisingly deep valley, going through a gate (a shortcut drops steeply to the right here) and following the ancient holloway down to a road.

Turn right at the road, passing the unexpected sight of a tourist information centre in the telephone box at Arosfa – one of an increasing number of red phone boxes enjoying an alternative afterlife – and slanting left across a stile after 100m to enter the **Pwll-y-Wrach Nature Reserve**. ▸ The very clear path passes two **waterfalls**, the second the more dramatic with a hard cap of limestone above softer, more easily eroded mudstones.

Just below the main waterfall there is a choice between a riverside path with a steep pull back up to the western entrance of the reserve, or a more easily graded trail that gains height steadily to reach the same point. Talgarth now lies 1km along the road, which passes the entrance to the Black Mountains business park, on a site that initially housed the Brecon & Radnor Lunatic Asylum – later the Mid Wales Hospital. The road then enters the town by crossing the recently reconstructed bridge over the **River Ennig**, which was responsible for serious flooding in **Talgarth** in 2008.

The waterfall and Witches Pool at Pwll-y-Wrach

A typical woodland reserve, Pwll-y-Wrach ('the Witches Pool') has wood anemones, celandines, wild garlic and bluebells in spring, summer visitors such as pied flycatchers and redstarts, and exotic fungi in autumn.

WALK 18
The Begwns

Start/Finish	Cattle grid above Croesfeilliog, 3km NW of Clyro (SO 181 445)
Distance	7km (4½ miles)
Ascent	175m (575ft)
Time	2–3hrs
Maps	Explorer 188 and Outdoor Leisure 13 both cover the whole of the walk
Public transport	The nearest buses call at Clyro, 3km from the start of the walk
Parking	Space for a few cars south of the cattle grid

This is a very easy walk with little climbing and a surface of springy green turf throughout, but set in sensational scenery, with the long ridges of the Brecon Beacons and the Black Mountains to the south and the gentler slopes of the hills of Mid Wales to the north.

Llowes Hall was formerly called Tir-y-Beddau – its name a reference to graves in the vicinity, possibly as a result of a battle.

Cross the road from the cattle grid, located on the north-eastern boundary of the Begwns common, and take the green track on the left, going back through the bracken and crossing the common, initially alongside the road but then diverging south-westwards to meet a narrow tarmac lane near Penyrheol. Turn right here, following the lane along the southern edge of the common until it swings left towards **Llowes Hall**. ◄ The way lies straight ahead here, climbing on a broad green track past the gaunt ruins of Bird's Nest Farm and continuing through the bracken, with the long, steep ridge of the Black Mountains away to the left.

The extensive upland heathland common of **The Begwns** was given to the National Trust in 1992. Largely bracken-covered, it also has areas of heather and gorse and it supports a very wide range of species, including brown hares, otters, heathland butterflies,

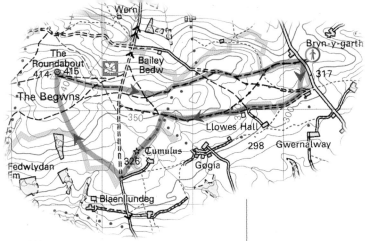

red kites,
buzzards and dragonflies. It is particularly important as a summer breeding ground for curlew, lapwing and golden plover. Burial cairns and a deserted
medieval village provide historical interest too.

Just beyond a gate giving a good view across the
18th-century farm buildings of Gogia, the path drops

*The broad green
track across the
common above
Gogia*

The Monks Pond may appear natural but it was actually created in the 1960s to control the water supply to Gogia Farm. Canada geese can be seen here, while there are also coot, mallard and great crested grebe.

down to negotiate a brief marshy area and swings left, still following the fence marking the southern boundary of the common, and now with the Monks Pond dominating the scene ahead. ◄ The route lies along the embankment just to the left of the **lake**, then climbs past a tumulus – easily picked out but covered in bracken – with a good view of the tree-covered summit of The Roundabout away to the right.

The path continues ahead as a wide grass rake with a wall to the left and more bracken to the right, with the distinctive high peaks of the Brecon Beacons dominating the skyline ahead. Cross a very narrow metalled lane close to a cattle grid, veer slightly right and ford a couple of minor streams, then climb fairly steeply with the edge of the common land still immediately on the left and a thin belt of woodland, the haunt of buzzards, coming up to the boundary of the common a little further ahead. Turn right just before the trees, following a narrow but very clear path through rough grassland and gorse, with stonechats perched on the latter in summer. ◄ Another swathe of bracken now needs to be crossed to arrive at a white trig pillar just before **The Roundabout**.

The deserted medieval village of Pentre Jack, with its house platforms and trackways, lies some way down the slope to the west.

> The **stone wall** enclosing The Roundabout was originally constructed in 1887 to protect trees planted on the summit of the Begwns to mark Queen Victoria's Golden Jubilee. It was substantially restored in 2000 to celebrate the Millennium, with a big circular stone seat added as a centrepiece at the summit of the hill, with its astonishing panorama over the Black Mountains, Brecon Beacons and Carmarthen Fan.

Walk around the stone wall to find a very obvious wide green path descending eastwards to a hollow just before the narrow lane is crossed again. Now aim for the narrow path climbing the hill just to the left (ignore the wider path to the right heading back to the Monks Pond). The buildings of the deserted farm at **Bailey Bedw** can be seen below to the left. Climb a little hillock with the stony

remains of a ring cairn to the left and take the middle of three clear paths, dropping down to ford a stream by a little pond.

The route, still on closely cropped turf, continues to take the same direction through the bracken, ignoring a succession of paths to left and right. Although the Black Mountain ridge still catches the eye to the south, the view to the north is now equally dramatic, with the long whaleback of Llanbedr Hill prominent beyond the lush Bachawy Valley and the village of Painscastle. ▶ Drop down to the corner of the common near Croesfeilliog Farm – one of several spots where the yellowhammer can be seen and heard in summer – and take the left-hand path, once again following the edge of the common on a very easy route back to the parking area by the cattle grid.

Painscastle and Llanbedr Hill from above Bailey Bedw

The motte and bailey castle at Painscastle was reconstructed in 1231, after the bloody battle here in 1198 in which Gwenwynwyn, Prince of Powys, was defeated by Geoffrey fitz Peter's English army.

WALK 19
Brechfa Pool

Start/Finish	Boughrood Bridge (SO 130 384)
Distance	10km (6 miles)
Ascent	450m (1475ft)
Time	3–4hrs
Map	Explorer 188
Public transport	Bus T4 provides a service roughly every two hours between Cardiff, Llyswen and Newtown, but not all buses undertake the whole journey
Parking	On-street parking in Boughrood and Llyswen

The rolling uplands north of the Brecon Beacons are little known but are well worth exploring, not least for the stunning views they offer of the higher hills. This walk takes in two of the best viewpoints, the all-round panorama from Mynydd Forest and the mountain view across the serene Brechfa Pool.

The first bridge over the Wye at Boughrood, replacing an early ford and ferry, dates from as recently as 1838–42, and the currently dilapidated tollhouse was added a few years later.

From **Boughrood Bridge** head west for a short distance to meet the A470, the main north-south road through Wales. ◄ The path straight across the A470 appears inviting on the map but is badly overgrown and disappears into a ravine, so instead turn left along the main road for 200m and climb the steps on the right to a stile. Cross two buttercup fields to a stile in the far corner, clamber over this to enter woodland and take the clear path (colonised by a stream for a while) that climbs steadily through the woods.

Cross a green forest road and ascend through bracken, brambles, rosebay willow-herb and foxgloves to reach clearfell on the left and young conifers on the right, with the views opening out nicely. Keep left when a somewhat indistinct path leaves to the right, climbing steadily with deer tracks on the path and excellent views of the Black Mountains behind. Buzzards and red kites are plentiful in the skies above, and the usual woodland suspects such as chiffchaffs can be heard in the trees.

Go through a metal gate and follow the clear track to the left, but quickly leave this to hug the right-hand edge of the common, aiming for a holly and two Scots pines that locate a drove between enclosed fields. Beyond this, take a thin path straight ahead to cross a minor road and head right, uphill, on a bridleway with good views of the Brecon Beacons to the left. Cross this and follow the bridleway to the right, heading across **Brechfa Common**.

The track hugs the left-hand edge of the common at Coedcochion and holds the same direction beyond the farm, aiming for a white post (one of several here, marking the line of a recently constructed oil pipeline) with the summit of Mynydd Forest immediately behind on the skyline.

Above the white post the way forward is delightful, curving up the summit slopes through chattering skylarks and meadow pipits on a broad path on springy

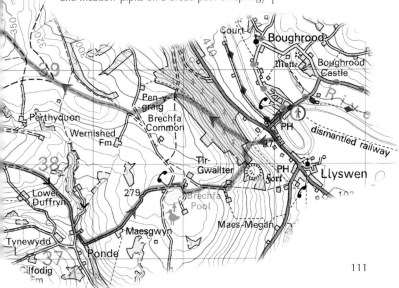

The bridleway leading to Mynydd Forest

turf. The summit itself is marked by a **trig pillar** with Welsh red dragons on each face.

> **Mynydd Forest** is an unremarkable hill of only 400m (1310ft), but it boasts an astonishing view, from Banc-y-Celyn in the north across the hidden Wye to Aberedw Rocks, Llanbedr Hill and the Begwns (with the small plantation at The Roundabout prominent); the Herefordshire hills, Lord Hereford's Knob and the Black Mountain scarp; Mynydd Troed, the Brecon Beacons and, in the distance, the Carmarthen Fan.

After drinking in the view keep straight ahead, taking the left-hand of two obvious paths and descending gradually across the open common towards **Nant-yr-arian**, avoiding this on the right and then swinging left, with good views of the lake below the house. Take a narrow path through bracken and drop down through gorse to cross a little valley – the crossing can be appallingly muddy after rain but the worst of the mud can be avoided by keeping right – and climb up to meet a minor road.

Follow the road down to the hamlet of **Ponde** and when the road curves right take the green lane on the left, veering left again to go quite steeply uphill towards **Maesgwyn**. The track is rocky in places and accompanied by a stream for a while, then it leads through a muddy gateway to reach a narrow tarmac lane heading past yet another white post denoting the route taken by the gas pipeline to arrive suddenly at **Brechfa Pool**.

Shallow and with varying water levels, **Brechfa Pool** is a magnet for wading birds on their spring and autumn migrations, and it also hosts breeding lapwing and black-headed gulls. Plantlife includes the rare pillwort together with pennyroyal and orange foxtail grass. The Calvinistic Methodist Bethesda Chapel, founded on the edge of common land in 1791, lies on the shores of the lake.

Bethesda Chapel, seen across the wide expanse of Brechfa Pool

Llyswen rectory and the Black Mountains on the descent to Boughrood

The hillfort, double banked and ditched, may be the site of the early-medieval 'white court' of Llyswen, where an early church is said to have been founded in the sixth century.

Head east from the pool, passing **Tir-Gwallter** on the left and crossing a delightful stretch of common land to go straight ahead, briefly on tarmac but then down a narrow bridleway with good views across the Wye Valley ahead. Quickly turn left, using a substantial stile and then zigzagging across two fields before dropping down, now with the massive **hillfort** of Pen-rhiw-wen in the woodland to the right. ◄

Below the north-western edge of the hillfort a stile gives access to woodland, with a thin path snaking diagonally down – ignore the path contouring the hillside. Leave the woodland over a further stile, aim half-left to the corner of the next field and go left to rejoin the outward route at the top of the two buttercup fields. Cross the two fields to reach the A470 in **Llyswen** (where John Thelwall, the hermit poet, was visited by Wordsworth and Coleridge in 1798) and turn left to return to **Boughrood Bridge**.

WALK 20

Llewellyn's Cave and Aberedw Rocks

Start/Finish	Seven Stars Inn, Aberedw (SO 080 472)
Distance	8km (5 miles)
Ascent	290m (950ft)
Time	2–3hrs
Map	Explorer 188
Public transport	None
Parking	Roadside parking in Aberedw

This route involves easy walking in the secret country above the Wye Valley south of Builth Wells, visiting a cave where a rebel Welsh prince is reputed to have spent his last night and exploring some of the many green tracks that criss-cross the common land around the low cliffs of Aberedw Rocks.

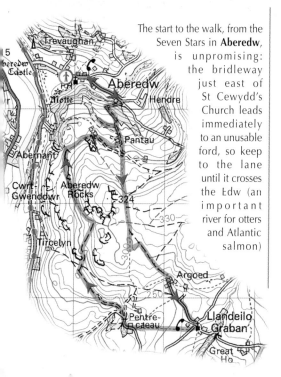

The start to the walk, from the Seven Stars in **Aberedw**, is unpromising: the bridleway just east of St Cewydd's Church leads immediately to an unusable ford, so keep to the lane until it crosses the Edw (an important river for otters and Atlantic salmon)

Inside Llewellyn's Cave – the slogan reads 'In memory of Llywelyn ap Gruffydd, Prince of Wales'

on a road bridge and then take the right-hand fork. Matters quickly improve on taking the track leading back to the right after 100m, which climbs steadily through woodland before swinging left to a gate. Go through this, then turn sharp right after 200m to go along the left-hand edge of a field, and cut through the bracken after a further 200m to discover Llewellyn's Cave in one of a number of rocky outcrops hidden in the trees.

Small and single-chambered, **Llewellyn's Cave** owes its fame solely to the events of 10 December 1282, when the Welsh prince Llywelyn ap Gruffydd, pursued by the forces of Edward I, is alleged to have spent the night in the cave before attempting to rejoin his troops to attack Builth Castle. But it was all in vain: on the following day Llywelyn and his followers were ambushed at nearby Cilmeri and put to the sword, effectively putting an end to Welsh independence.

Back on the main track, climb steadily until just after the ruined farmhouse and attached bakehouse at **Pantau**, with its resident tawny owls, a path leads through high bracken into a bowl beneath another line of rocky bluffs. Take the obvious green track straight ahead, ascending a shallow dry valley, to reach a delightful area of heather moorland backed by a low rock escarpment above a little pond, with a fine view of the long ridge of the Black Mountains to the left.

Swing left past the pond, on a broad green path on springy turf that is easy to follow, now with the Wye Valley down to the right and the ridge of Banc-y-Celyn beyond it. Some distance after the pond a path leads off to the left, but there is a confusion of paths here; it is easier to stay on the main track across the common and, when an enclosed field appears ahead, walk round to the left of this to pick up the track leading directly to the farm complex at **Argoed**. The route then continues as a tarmac lane as far as the old, low church at **Llandeilo Graban**. ▶

The tiny settlement at Llandeilo Graban (St Teilo's Church by the corn marigolds) consisted only of a church, farm and cottage, and even in the early 19th century was served only by often impassable private roads.

Take the lane going south-west from the church, then turn right on a path that crosses a number of small fields to rejoin the lane by the handsome 15th-century farmhouse at **Pentrecaeau Uchaf**. The lane, often occupied by sheep, zigzags down below the farm. Ignore the track leading off to New House on the right, but after a further 50m, at an impromptu parking spot, take the thin and initially indistinct path through the bracken on the right.

The path becomes much clearer as it dips down, swings left to climb a small slope and then takes a level course across the common, merging with a broader track and leading to the seasonal lake at Henllyn Mawr. ▶ Skirt the lake (if it exists!) on its right-hand side and turn right, going gently uphill, at its head. As the green track approaches an escarpment a lesser path goes off to the left; carry straight on for a few metres to inspect a boundary stone on the right-hand side of the track, but then return to the junction and take the smaller path,

Henllyn Mawr is the largest of several small lakes on the common that shrink or disappear in summer. Known as mawn pools, they support important populations of the threatened fairy shrimp.

117

The seasonal lake at Henllyn Mawr

The boundary stone – one of several on the common – is clearly dated 1882 and bears the initials JRB for Joseph Russell Bailey of the Glanusk estate.

then merge left onto a broader path skirting beneath the escarpment with its sandstone tors. ◄

The path continues below the crest of the **Aberedw Rocks** for some while before climbing slightly to cut through the rocks at the head of a deep side-valley and continue as a path running along the edge of the common, with a wire fence to the left. A prominent pond down to the left holds wildfowl in summer. Zigzag left and right below a scree slope, pass the entrance to Pen-y-gareg Farm and cut across the common to rejoin the outward route just above the abandoned **Pantau farmhouse**. The track now heads back down the hillside to the lane leading back to **Aberedw**, worth exploring for the remains of its two castles, an early motte and a 12th-century stone-built Welsh fortress

WALK 21

Llandeilo Hill and Twm Tobacco's Grave

Start/Finish	Seven Stars Inn, Aberedw (SO 080 472)
Distance	12km (7½ miles)
Ascent	510m (1675ft)
Time	4–5hrs
Map	Explorer 188
Public transport	None
Parking	Roadside parking in Aberedw

This is a spectacular ridge walk across one of the largest areas of heather moorland remaining in the Welsh borders, with every chance of seeing the elusive red grouse. Beyond the simple grave of the enigmatic Twm Tobacco the route descends into the scenic Edw valley.

From the Seven Stars in **Aberedw** take the valley road past St Cewydd's Church and over the Afon Edw, then turn immediately right on a narrow lane that rises steadily, with improving views across the Edw valley to Aberedw Hill and, to its left, the

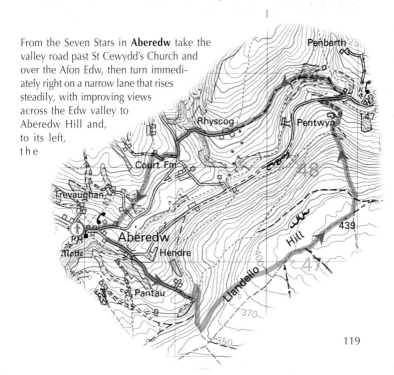

Morning mist on the track above Pentre-moel Farm

Wye Valley below Builth Wells. When the slope eases, the lane to Pentre-moel Farm leaves to the left and the way ahead immediately becomes a rough track, alternately grassy and stony, eventually rising to a field gate. Leave the main track (which goes on to pass the platform on which the forerunner of the present Pentre-moel farmhouse stood) 50m after the gate, turning sharply right to climb obliquely across common land below white limestone crags.

Ignore a broad crossing path and continue to climb on a grassy track, which zigzags onto the plateau at a walkers' crossroads marked by a recumbent waymark post. It is worth going some 10m beyond this and then searching for the Rhiw Gwydd boundary stone on the left, but the route turns left at the crossroads, taking a broad green path through the bracken, with the sound of skylarks very common from March throughout the summer. ◄

The Rhiw Gwydd stone dates from the 19th century and is inscribed 'W de W' – after the de Winton family, who were local landowners.

The path undulates gently across the common, now cutting through heather moorland, with the Edw valley spread out below rocky outcrops to the left and a distant view of hills such as the Begwns on the right, with the Black Mountains still further away. Closer at hand on the right are the low mounds of peat stands (hinting at earlier uses of the common), with Farlen Pool – the first of the mawn pools encountered on this walk – a little way to the right of the path.

> The **mawn pools** of Radnorshire are nutrient-rich seasonal ponds that support unusual wildlife, including the only known Welsh population of the rare fairy shrimp and a number of uncommon water beetles. The ponds are actually small, shallow basin mires – some no longer with much visible water – on deep peat deposits, edged by bulrushes and often overgrown by heather.

The walking is easy and exhilarating, but identifiable landmarks on the summit ridge of **Llandeilo Hill** are few and far between and there is a plethora of tracks and paths that don't always follow the exact line shown on the OS map, so it is important to keep to a north-easterly direction along the ridge to skirt a depression, swing left and then right on a track coming up from Blaen Henllan and skirt the bigger Glannau Pool in a heathery hollow with shooting butts beyond and to the left. The heather here has been managed for grouse shooting, with strips of mown heather at periodic intervals, and there is a healthy population of red grouse, which career away across the moor on a low, frantic flight path as soon as they're disturbed.

Follow the waymark pointing straight on just after Glannau Pool, crossing the heather moor with Llanbwchllyn Lake – a combined fishing lake and nature reserve with unusually rich fen vegetation – coming into view on the right. Another mawn pool can be seen away to the left, while the track itself follows a level course along the ridge to arrive at a waymark post, another low boundary stone and the simple cross and heap of stones marking Twm Tobacco's Grave.

> Opinions differ as to the status of **Twm Tobacco**, who was possibly a 17th-century packman or

Twm Tobacco's grave on the ridge of Llandeilo Hill

travelling salesman, buried here at a favourite resting place; perhaps an itinerant or drunkard who died of exposure in this bleak, isolated spot; or perhaps a cattle rustler, sheep stealer or thief who was hanged from a gibbet and then buried on unconsecrated territory at this lonely crossroads of former packhorse routes.

Turn left just beyond the grave, following a narrow and somewhat indistinct path along the edge of the heather and dropping down to cross a broad green path and descend quite steeply through bracken. The path quickly improves, passing the remains of an ancient field boundary and reaching a gate at the edge of the common. ◄ Go through the gate and veer right, then turn sharply left along a broad farm track that swings right and left, crosses a mercifully brief sea of mud and arrives in the farmyard at **Pentwyn**. Turn right here and follow the track down to the valley road.

The low bank enclosing the old field had been abandoned by the 19th century, but it survives as evidence of more intensive cultivation of these high hills in medieval times.

It is possible to follow the road back alongside the delightful Afon Edw to Aberedw, but the more interesting

option turns right along the road for 300m and then goes left, climbing the hillslope to reach a delightful, tree-lined byway that cuts through woodland and then makes straight for **Rhyscog Farm**. Beyond the farm a narrow lane drops down to cross a stream and then rises to a road junction. Turn left here, then right along another track as far as Pen-y-bryn, with a final left turn here to traverse through a series of fields below Trevaughan – historically the most important of the valley farms – to reach the road leading back to the church and Seven Stars in **Aberedw**.

River terraces by the Afon Edw

WALK 22
Builth and Banc-y-Celyn

Start/Finish	Lion Hotel, Builth Wells (SO 042 510)
Distance	14km (9 miles)
Ascent	495m (1625ft)
Time	4–6hrs
Map	Explorer 188
Public transport	Builth Wells has seven services a day on service T4 between Cardiff, Brecon and Newtown, and five services a day on bus 44 to Llandrindod Wells
Parking	Limited on-street parking and a large pay-and-display car park at The Groe, by the river

This is a long and exhilarating traverse of the high country south of Builth Wells and west of the Wye, with far-reaching views and easy walking across a vast tract of common land, with prehistoric monuments and an attractive upland lake.

A Norman bastide settlement, Builth was defended by one of Edward I's border fortresses, with a massive motte and two baileys.

Take the lane on the right-hand side of the Lion Hotel in **Builth Wells**, then go left (signposted) up a narrow paved path and over a stile to reach the base of the castle ramparts. ◄ Climb up to the castle ditch and follow this or the outer rampart down to the left, eventually dropping down to cross a stile onto a suburban road. Turn right here, then left onto Newry Road, which is equally suburban until the edge of town is reached at Tanhouse Bridge, but then becomes a narrow and little-used country lane.

Beyond Sunnybank, where the green ridge of Banc-y-Celyn is seen for the first time, the way lies straight ahead when the road turns right, now following a lane that ends abruptly at the crossing of the Afon Duhonw. The choice is between a solid footbridge or the ford alongside, both leading to a gravelly track that climbs to reach a country lane just beyond the path to **Pwllgwyn**. Turn sharp left onto a green lane at this point, with sudden tremendous views back down to Builth Wells on the left and the bumpy

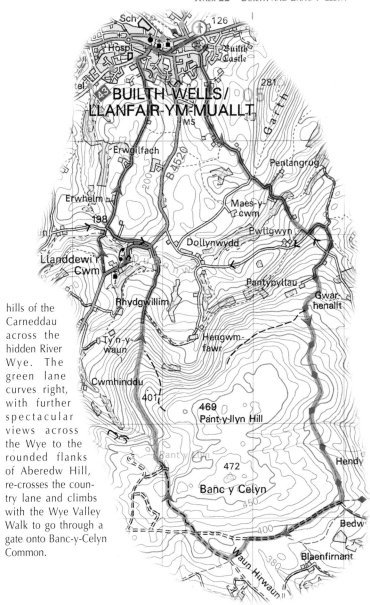

hills of the
Carneddau
across the
hidden River
Wye. The
green lane
curves right,
with further
spectacular
views across
the Wye to the
rounded flanks
of Aberedw Hill,
re-crosses the coun-
try lane and climbs
with the Wye Valley
Walk to go through a
gate onto Banc-y-Celyn
Common.

The view north into the Wye Valley from Banc-y-Celyn

The fine upland common of **Banc-y-Celyn** is now home only to sheep and mountain ponies, although it was once more heavily populated and has a number of historic features, including a stone circle and abandoned farmsteads. Part of a massive upland plateau, it lies between the Wye and Duhonw rivers and is an important wildlife site, with skylarks, wheatears, linnets and meadow pipits everywhere in summer, and ravens, buzzards and red kites overhead.

Follow the Wye Valley Walk across the left-hand edge of the common for an easy, exhilarating 2km, initially using a wide green path through bracken and later following a less well-defined path, fording a little stream and climbing again with the village of Aberedw down to the left and the superb sight of the Black Mountains ridge ahead. When a fence bars the way ahead, turn right (the Wye Valley Walk departs to the left here) and follow the course of the old drove road, which came across Mynydd Epynt on its way from Cwm Owen down into the Wye Valley. The drove is wide and green until a rutted track comes in from the left, at which point it becomes more worn for a short distance. Take the left fork when the path divides, quickly reaching a narrow tarmac road. The route goes right here, but it is worth going straight ahead for 100m to see the Twyn y Big cairn at the top of the slope. ▶

Follow the road gently uphill for some 400m until it curves left; take the obvious green path going straight ahead here, passing to the right of a small hillock and then cresting a rise with the extraordinary sight down to the left in early summer of a former lake bed colonised by bright white bog cotton. Around the next corner, beyond a rock outcrop, is the equally attractive mountain lake of **Pant-y-Llyn**. ▶ Take the path to the right of the lake to find a fenced enclosure containing the scanty remains of the Pant-y-Llyn farmstead – abandoned in the early 19th century and now indicated only by boundary banks, a holloway and just a hint of the old farmhouse.

A steep grassy path drops steeply down from Pant-y-Llyn's outflow to cross a deep valley and climb gently, now as a magnificent green path running through bilberry and gorse, with every chance of seeing red kites and ravens at close quarters. The view ahead is almost entirely of green rolling hills, but it also includes the Royal Welsh Showground beyond Builth Wells. The path descends easily to a gate at the edge of the common; go straight ahead here on a lane that is initially grassy but

The cairn dates from the Bronze Age and has three remaining upright stones, although the site has been severely disturbed over the years.

The lake covers 3ha (7 acres) and is now operated as a coarse fishery with wild carp a particular attraction; it is superbly situated in remote surroundings at the head of a narrow valley.

The superb green lane from the former Pant-y-Llyn farm towards Builth Wells

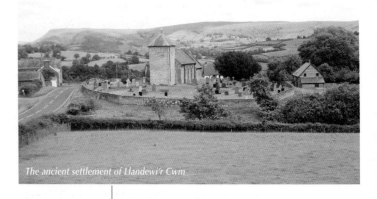

The ancient settlement of Llandewi'r Cwm

A tucking-mill and dye works powered by a waterwheel stood to the north-east of the farm, but very little remains to identify this outpost of woollen manufacturing.

becomes stony as it passes Wern-wyn Farm. ◄ The B4520 is reached just beyond the farm, with a choice of routes.

Alternative route via Llandewi'r Cwm

The longer alternative takes the B-road past the simple but evocative church at **Llandewi'r Cwm** in its ancient sub-circular churchyard, finds an overgrown bridleway dropping down to a high, solid footbridge over the Afon Duhonw, and climbs a damp track up to the road junction.

The main route lies straight ahead, steeply up a narrow lane to a road junction (where the alternative route rejoins the main). Take the tarmac road going north to Cnwc-y-llo, with good views back to the long ridge of Banc-y-Celyn, and on reaching the farm keep straight ahead on an enclosed track. There is a good view over Builth Wells, with the River Wye prominent beyond, before a steep descent over exposed bedrock leads to the edge of the old market town, with an easy stroll along the main street of the old spa town, which had sulphur and saline wells, leading back to the Lion Hotel in **Builth Wells**.

WALK 23
Cors y Llyn

Start/Finish	Cors y Llyn car park (SO 015 557)
Distance	8km (5 miles)
Ascent	110m (360ft)
Time	2–3hrs
Map	Explorer 200
Public transport	Bus 45 runs three times a day (twice in school holidays) between Builth Wells and Newbridge-on-Wye, passing 1km (½ mile) from Cors y Llyn
Parking	Small car park at the entrance to Cors y Llyn National Nature Reserve

Cors y Llyn is an unmissable highlight of the upper Wye Valley, a superb National Nature Reserve based on the only quaking bog in Wales, with a unique geological and botanical history. The walk also takes in the site of a Roman fortlet on the banks of the Wye, and an excellent byway overlooking the green hill country typical of Mid Wales.

From the car park at **Cors y Llyn** head down the green path towards the lake (better still, in early summer, follow the mown path through the field on the left, which is full of orchids) and choose between turning right to follow the public footpath or left around the lake. The former option leads to a gate and another choice: either straight on or left, in both cases on a boardwalk. The latter runs past the lake (sometimes

Luxuriant vegetation around the pool at Cors y Llyn

a hobby can be seen here hunting for dragonflies) to join the boardwalk halfway round the reserve.

> The National Nature Reserve of **Cors y Llyn** consists of two basin mires scoured out by glacial activity, with a drier ridge, a herb-rich meadow and areas of wet woodland. The vegetation in the mires grew out over deep pools to form a mat, which floats on the water surface. Stunted Scots pines, only two metres high, struggle to survive, while bog mosses, cotton grass, round-leaved sundew and the attractive, uncommon marsh cinquefoil thrive in the wet conditions.

The boardwalks, which lie only an inch or two above the water and can be swamped after heavy rain, are remarkably extensive, but there are seats at regular intervals for those who want to drink in the scene, from the plentiful birdlife – ranging from tree pipits and willow warblers in summer to woodcock and snipe in winter – to the remarkably varied vegetation. Eventually the two boardwalks join again to pass an area of deep pools, sodden sphagnum and colourful mosses and lichens.

A gate now signals the end of the boardwalk and leads into a field full of anthills covered in clumps of tiny white flowers. A thin path winds between the anthills, making for a stile to the left and a field abandoned to bracken and nettles. Follow the clear path to the left through the next field, go straight across another pasture to a gate, and take the middle of three paths – actually a pleasant green lane – through woodland, with a modern barn to the right.

When the woodland falls away to the left it is replaced with a delightful flower-rich hay meadow, often frequented by groups of red kites prospecting for small mammals. The lane runs past this field and on to **Smithfield Farm** – an old farmhouse arranged around a courtyard, with stone-built house, stable, cowhouse and cartshed – before rising on a tarmac lane to meet the old A470 at Little Smithfield. Turn right along the old main road, now superseded by a modern bypass a further field away and little more than a country lane.

Stunted Scots pines alongside the boardwalk at Cors y Llyn

The green lane to Smithfield Farm

Another right turn leads onto the narrow lane sign-posted to Caerwnon Park – a surprisingly suburban rash of retirement homes in the grounds of the mock timber-framed **Caerwnon House**. The lane continues through well-wooded and gently undulating country, eventually arriving at a bridge over the former Mid Wales Railway. ◀ Just beyond the bridge, turn left on a bridleway that runs through **Penmincae Farm**, swerves left and then right and becomes much less well defined as it drops down to the river, with the site of a Roman fortlet just to the left.

An unlikely site for a Roman camp, **Penmincae** guarded the point at which the fairly minor Roman road from Beulah to Castle Collen near Llandrindod Wells forded the Wye. A rectangular enclosure on slightly higher ground is best seen from aerial photographs, although first-century Samian ware has been discovered within the ramparts. The road to Castle Collen is thought to have run north-east, although the byway to Craig-goch-fach, which forms part of this walk, is also interestingly straight and potentially Roman in origin.

The view to Llysdinam from above Craig-goch-fach

Return to the railway bridge and go through the metal gate just to the east (a signpost would be helpful here). The route is clearly defined as a byway on the map, but is less obvious on the ground; nevertheless it is an easy and enjoyable walk, at first on a clear track but then following fainter signs alongside the left-hand edge of successive fields. ▶ The byway rises steadily through a number of gates, with improving views across the Wye Valley to the west, while to the east the low volcanic hills of the Builth inlier are equally prominent.

The cattle here are likely to be pedigree Welsh Blacks – a breed indelibly associated with the cattle droves of Mid Wales.

When the plateau is reached there is a glimpse of the church at Newbridge-on-Wye slightly to the left, with the country mansion of Llysdinam even more prominent on the hillslopes further left. **Cors y Llyn** is now visible down to the right as the broad track approaches the farm at Craig-goch-fach, then swings right to return to the nature reserve car park.

133

WALK 24
Shaky Bridge

Start/Finish	Shaky Bridge, 3km (2 miles) east of Llandrindod Wells (SO 084 612)
Distance	12km (7½ miles)
Ascent	420m (1380ft)
Time	3–4hrs
Map	Explorer 200
Public transport	The nearest buses and trains call at Llandrindod Wells, 3km (2 miles) from the start of the walk
Parking	Small car park at Shaky Bridge

This is a very varied walk, taking in the dramatic outcrop at Cefnllys and its two short-lived castles, the valley of the Ithon (a major tributary of the Wye) and the hidden but remarkably scenic volcanic hills of the Builth inlier, together with a slew of prehistoric and medieval earthworks and monuments.

The nature reserve includes wet alder and ash with a hazel understorey, and hosts an impressive variety of wildflowers together with breeding birds such as pied flycatcher, redstart and garden warbler.

Before crossing **Shaky Bridge**, take a side trip through the kissing gate into the Bailey Einon Nature Reserve, with its trails and boardwalk through riverside woodland. ◀ Now cross Shaky Bridge, replaced in 2011 and now providing a very firm crossing of the River Ithon, in contrast to the original ford and an early primitive plank bridge.

Turn right 30m after the bridge to cross a hidden stile and climb steeply, over tree roots and even a rock step, to find a superb grassy path through bracken as the slope eases somewhat, although frequent rest stops may still be needed to admire the scenery. The path rises quickly to reach the plateau on top of Castle Bank, with the later of two adjacent castles immediately ahead and the second a short distance across the hilltop.

The first stone castle at **Cefnllys** was erected in the 1240s by Roger Mortimer, the first Baron Mortimer of Wigmore in Herefordshire, during his long

The Ithon valley from the slopes of Castle Bank

struggle for supremacy in these border lands with Llywelyn ap Gruffydd, Prince of Wales. The castle was destroyed by Llywelyn in 1262, but Mortimer replaced it with a more substantial castle at the south end of the hilltop around 1273. This, too, was relatively short-lived, being sacked in 1295 and finally burnt by Glyndŵr in 1406.

Stroll across to the north-eastern edge of the plateau from the earlier castle to look down on St Michael's, the parish church of the deserted medieval village of Cefnllys. ▶ A track now leads towards the farm complex at **Neuadd**, but leave this to cut steeply down alongside a hedge and reach a green track that rises gently to reach and pass through the farm buildings. Neuadd stands within the deer park associated with Cefnllys Castle and the Court Leet of Cefnllys borough was still held here in the 19th century.

Beyond the farm the track becomes a quiet metalled lane, with swallows on the wires and red kites hovering low overhead as it passes Neuadd Isaf and its pedigree Limousin cattle, skirts a long narrow buttercup field and

The church has a 15th-century screen but it has been heavily restored, while the fields around the church contain traces of the 25 burgage plots of the medieval borough.

arrives at a
road junction near
Cwm. A bridleway leaves to the right through
a red gate here, and although it is not waymarked it is
accepted as a right of way and roughly defined on the
ground as it heads across three fields towards the road
near Brynthomas.

Cross the modern road bridge over the river north of
Brynthomas (the stone abutments of its predecessor still
stand alongside), with the chance of seeing goosanders in
the waters below. Once past the farm, swing left onto a
narrow lane, with good views of the curious low hills of
Llandegley Rocks and Bwlch-y-cefn straight ahead. The
lane is little used, with a grass strip down the middle as it

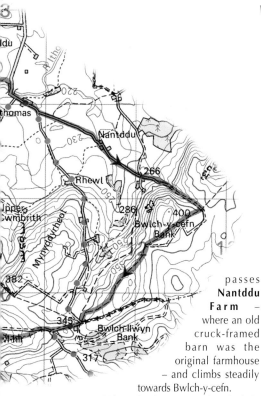

passes
**Nantddu
Farm** –
where an old
cruck-framed
barn was the
original farmhouse
– and climbs steadily
towards Bwlch-y-cefn.

When the lane turns sharply left,
keep straight ahead on a gravelly track climbing a thinly
wooded valley to reach the ridge near the Sarn Pool. Turn
right, following a bridleway that is slightly indistinct at
first across a huge upland pasture but becomes a delightful grassy path cutting through bracken to reach a stand
of conifers where the Hundred House road cuts across
the ridge.

The route follows the road for 400m until it bends
left; go straight on here, following a byway as a rough
track across the upland pastures of **Pawl-hir**. ▶ The track,
now with good views south over Gilwern Hill, curves left
and then right and is flanked by gorse and small trees as

This is one of the
many old drove roads
that took cattle, sheep
and even geese and
turkeys from Mid
Wales to markets in
Hereford and further
afield.

137

it approaches two curiously shaped **ponds** – the nearer of which has Canada geese, tufted ducks, little grebe and raucous breeding black-headed gulls in summer.

The byway continues as a wonderful green lane with astonishing views of the unknown green bowl below the hills east of Llandrindod, with Castle Bank and its two castles increasingly prominent. Earthen field banks to the right are followed by the sad remains on the right of the farmstead and attached cowhouse at Pen-rhiw Frank, while to the left there are unseen standing stones and the more visible remains of the Iron Age promontory fort on Careg-wiber Bank.

The green lane now begins to descend steeply, with the hills of Mid Wales directly ahead, then swings sharply right to descend above Bank House towards the farms at **Llanoley**, now as an enclosed track that is at first gravelly and then concreted as it curves left. Go through a gate on the right at the bottom of the hill to take a green lane – damp after heavy rain – then go through another gate to cross common land on a superb green path.

> **Llanoley** is now a quiet backwater, but from the 17th century onwards it was a centre of Quaker religion, with marriages celebrated here and a small parcel of land leased at a peppercorn rent for 999 years in 1714 and used as a burial plot. The Quakers of Llanoley were persecuted for their beliefs, too, with both Mary Bevan and 80-year-old Ann Thomas incarcerated in Presteigne gaol.

The path runs between areas of bracken and bluebells, and through mixed deciduous woodland with a stream to the left, and with rabbits, squirrels, song thrushes and warblers all in evidence. Finally, the old green track drops down steadily through still more bracken to go through a gate and onto a forestry road – somewhat bizarrely surfaced with half-bricks and rubble – to arrive back at the car park at **Shaky Bridge**.

THE UPPER WYE
Newbridge-on-Wye to Plynlimon

Looking down on the source of the Wye (Walk 30)

WALK 25
Above the Elan Valley reservoirs

Start/Finish	Northern end of Garreg-ddu Reservoir (SN 915 673)
Distance	12km (7½ miles)
Ascent	435m (1425ft)
Time	3–4hrs
Map	Explorer 200
Public transport	None
Parking	Small car park at the northern end of Garreg-ddu Reservoir

This is a strenuous exploration of part of the Elenydd, a huge wildlife-rich area of open moorland that is sometimes referred to as Wales' 'green desert'. Ancient cairns on remote hilltops, a Roman marching camp and views of the Craig Goch and Penygarreg reservoirs provide added interest.

Head back across the bridge from the **car park**, with a view of the tumbling river below the Penygarreg dam to the left, then go through a gate by the red telephone box to curve left, briefly on the Elan Woodland Walk. The route quickly turns sharply right, before a footbridge, and climbs steeply to reach a narrow lane. Turn right along the lane, but when this bends to the right take the stony track on the left, gaining height steadily and soon emerging above the trees, with redstarts and warblers for company in summer.

> The chain of **reservoirs** in the Elan Valley is the result of the damming of the Elan and Claerwen rivers to provide drinking water for Birmingham. Construction of the four reservoirs (Craig Goch, Penygarreg, Garreg-ddu and Caban-coch) was completed in 1904, by which time farms, cottages, a church and a chapel lay under the rising waters. Water is carried by gravity to Frankley Reservoir near Birmingham in the Elan aqueduct.

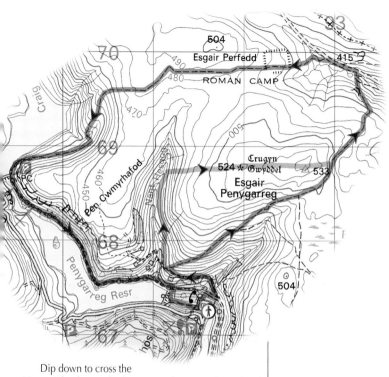

Dip down to cross the
Nant y Blymbren, climb again and pass to the right of
Penygarreg Farm, with a brief glimpse across the reser-
voir. There is now a choice of routes.

*White quartz rocks
on the lonely summit
of Crugyn Gwyddel*

The cairn was reused as a boundary marker for the monastic Cwmdeuddwr Grange and as a beacon site, which explains the strikingly white quartzite rocks at its centre.

Defended by a bank and ditch to the south, close to another tumulus, Crugyn Ci boasts an amazingly wide summit panorama including Radnor Forest, the peaks of Drygarn Fawr and Plynlimon and the Wye Valley and Rhayader.

The camp measures 240m by 270m, its boundaries indicated by a turf-covered rampart, although this is hard to discern on the ground. It was in use only briefly before being abandoned in favour of more hospitable sites.

Alternative route via Crugyn Gwyddel

A more adventurous alternative takes a less sharp right turn than the main route and contours above the **Nant Hesgog**, at first on a clear track but later following a thin path some way above the stream. As the valley narrows, climb out to the right and head east across heather moorland to the Bronze Age burial cairn **Crugyn Gwyddel** ('the little mound of the Irishmen'). ◄

Continue in the same direction towards the summit ridge of Crugyn Ci, festooned with concrete posts marking the boundary of Birmingham Corporation's Elan estate and with an **OS trig pillar** defining the top as 533m (1749ft). ◄ Descend gradually from the summit, passing between little rocky outcrops and eventually rejoining the main route on the bridleway coming over from Penygarreg, here a green track passing through rough grassland and bilberry.

The easier main route turns sharply right to follow a bridleway, which crosses a couple of fields to reach the moorland edge and then climbs steadily across the southern slopes of **Esgair Penygarreg**, with the alternative route rejoining the main following its descent from Crugyn Ci.

Cross the Nant Gwynllyn just above an attractive waterfall to reach the old mountain road between Rhayader and Aberystwyth – formerly the main turnpike route between the two towns until it was superseded by the current valley route in the 19th century.

Turn left along the road for 400m, then pause by a bridleway sign to survey the site of the **Roman marching camp** on the hillside ahead. ◄ Take the bridleway over stepping stones, veer left at a sheepfold and climb on the rutted track past the marching camp. As the slope eases, it is worth glancing back across the mountain road to the long ridge of Esgair Dderw, with the slim pillar of the Maen Serth standing stone clearly visible.

The path becomes less well defined and braids in places as it crosses the rounded southern shoulder of **Esgair Perfedd**; it is crucial to take a course that gradually curves left to head south-westward across the plateau (a

The path through the rock cutting on the old railway alongside Penygarreg Reservoir

compass or GPS is particularly useful here, especially in mist, since there are few landmarks and there are paths not marked on the map that lead too far to the right). The key is to stay south of the upper reaches of the Nant Gors-y-nod valley and descend into Cwm Garw on the eastern shore of Craig Goch Reservoir, with the path improving and becoming a pleasant green trod.

Beyond a ford the path becomes stony as it contours above the reservoir, with the Craig Goch dam and its curved retaining wall visible ahead, and a small beach below on the shores of the reservoir. Keep straight ahead beyond the dam, now on the Elan Valley Trail – a stony all-purpose route following the trackbed of a railway that was built to service the construction of the dams and then quickly dismantled.

The rocky bluffs of Craig yr Allt-goch rise above sessile oak woodland rich in lichens to the left of the track, while **Penygarreg Reservoir**, with its attractive wooded island, lies below on the right. A rock cutting betrays the origin of the route as a railway, while beyond this a Baroque valve tower surmounts the Penygarreg dam. Leave the Elan Valley Trail immediately after the dam, going through a small gate and dropping quickly down a narrow path, crossing the river Elan on a footbridge and turning left to follow the river downstream to the **car park** and the end of an exhilarating walk.

WALK 26
Drygarn Fawr

Start/Finish	Car park at Llanerch Cawr, at the western end of Dol-y-mynach Reservoir (SN 900 616)
Distance	15km (9½ miles)
Ascent	460m (1510ft)
Time	4–6hrs
Map	Explorer 200
Public transport	None
Parking	Small car park at Llanerch Cawr

This is not a walk to be undertaken lightly, since the plateau is remote, has few landmarks and is very boggy after rain. But on a fine day it is exhilarating: the views are extraordinary and the high moorland, wild and untamed, contrasts with fascinating sylvan valleys.

Take the lane running down from the **car park** to cross the Afon Claerwen and climb towards Llanerch Cawr Farm, but just before the farm – its core a classic 16th-century Welsh longhouse – turn sharp right onto a signposted bridleway heading for Rhiwnant. Quickly turn left and go through a gate to reach the open hillside, climbing gently on a broad stony track below the cliffs of Craig Llanerch-y-Cawr (red kites can often be seen circling above the crags here) and with the classic U-shaped glaciated Rhiwnant valley down to the right.

The grey stony track rises alongside the **Nant Paradwys**, but when it veers violently left take the thin path going straight ahead through a gate (there is a waymark post but it is been prostrate for some time). Down to the right the Nant Paradwys tumbles down some attractive waterslides, while the narrow path alternates between grassy and rocky, with occasional damp patches. The path breasts a rise and enters the 'green desert', with little but rounded green hills in view for a while.

Bl
Rhiw

The route swings left, away from the stream, to avoid the worst of the boggy areas, then crosses a damp level area (the tussocky grass to the left provides drier going) before rising gently, now on a pleasant green path with a distinct mountain feel. Beyond the upper reaches of the Nant Paradwys the way lies across level, featureless moorland to the grassy col at **Bwlch y Ddau Faen**. Remnant pools lie to the right, while straight ahead there is a sudden dramatic view of the distant Brecon Beacons. ▶

It is important to veer sharply right at the stone circle, climbing the grassy slope with the aid of sheep tracks until the unmistakable twin cairns on the summit of Drygarn Fawr come into view ahead. The cairn on the summit of Gorllwyn is now visible to the east, while a similar cairn on the subsidiary summit of **Carreg yr Ast** is a useful landmark away to the north. The chatter of skylarks is constant in summer, while ravens wheel acrobatically overhead.

Bwlch y Ddau Faen translates as 'pass of the two stones' yet there are four upright stones here. It has been argued that they're the remains of a stone circle, but it is more likely they marked a cattle droving route across the pass.

The summit ridge of Drygarn Fawr from the western cairn

The concrete posts marked the boundary of Birmingham Corporation's Elan estate, since gifted to the Elan Valley Trust.

A line of low concrete posts marks the approximate line of the 'official' path, but in truth any number of sheep tracks offer just as easy a crossing of the moorland, with its peat hags and occasional stands of bilberry. ◄ The path swings right to tackle the steeper final ascent of **Drygarn Fawr**, still aiming unerringly for the very prominent summit cairns.

> One of the most isolated summits in Wales, **Drygarn Fawr** rises from a sea of wet moorland, its grassy saddleback ridge a dry oasis. At each end of the summit ridge there is a huge beehive cairn, constructed from the stones of earlier Bronze Age cairns and capped by white quartz stones. The panorama is stunning, the 'green desert of Wales' all around and Plynlimon, the Brecon Beacons and Preseli Hills on the horizon.

Head north-east from the summit cairn, aiming for the valley of the Nant yr Ast, which is clearly in view across a largely trackless grassy moorland with areas of bilberry, dwarf heather and mosses. Keep the peat hags to the left, using intermittent sheep tracks where they help but generally making a beeline for the valley and passing close to the site of a rectangular stone hut – a former 'hafodty' or shepherd's summer dwelling. Take care on the steeper slopes in the valley itself, step across the stream and follow a thin path down the eastern bank to the confluence with the Rhiwnant stream.

The path along the Rhiwnant is easy to follow, although there are some tricky crossings of tributary streams and some rocky steps, and at one point the path rises above a delightful little gorge. The stream swings right, with the path some distance away across an open grassy area and the remains of the Nant-y-Garw lead mine clearly in view in a little ravine beyond this. ▶ Across the valley the gently descending line of the mine access track – blasted out of the steep slopes of Craig Rhiwnant – is a prominent landscape feature.

Cross a boggy area to arrive at a second set of mine workings – of the **Dalrhiw copper and lead mine** on the near bank and the Nant-y-car South copper, lead and zinc mine across the stream. ▶ Avoid the temptation to take the prominent track rising to the right and instead drop down to the riverbank, following an intermittent path through more wet ground to the confluence of the Rhiwnant and the Nant Paradwys. The crossing of the Nant Paradwys can be a challenge after rain, but once accomplished a gently rising track leads up to the track used on the outward route. Turn left here to return to the **car park**.

The Nant-y-Garw mine was prospected in 1877 and was worked for only 20 years, but the remains are extensive, including the shaft, wheelpit, crushing mill, barracks and mine office.

The crusher house, wheelpit and ore bins of the Nant-y-car mine, opened in the late 18th century, are particularly impressive.

The Rhiwnant valley from the ruins of the Dalrhiw mine

WALK 27

Gilfach Farm

Start/Finish	Marteg Bridge car park (SN 953 714)
Distance	6km (3½ miles)
Ascent	180m (590ft)
Time	2hrs
Map	Explorer 200
Public transport	Infrequent bus services between Rhayader and Aberystwyth or Llanidloes run via Pont Marteg, very close to the car park
Parking	Car park just off the A470 north of Rhayader, on the St Harmon road

This is a very short walk but one worth taking slowly in order to savour the wildlife and the sense of antiquity on an old, unimproved upland farm. The farm is now Gilfach Nature Reserve, centred on a wonderful medieval longhouse and with a rich variety of habitats including hay meadows, wetland, upland pasture and woodland.

From the car park near **Pont Marteg**, go a few steps back to the A470, turn left to cross the Afon Marteg and immediately turn left again, around the end of a crash barrier and over a stile to join the Gilfach Nature Trail as it snakes along the hillside above the south bank of the river before crossing a little bridge and dropping down steps onto the trackbed of the former Mid Wales Railway. ◀ As the railway track approaches a shallow but rather boggy cutting (which provides an excellent habitat for glow worms) the path rises slightly to the left, running through heather, gorse and bracken with excellent views across the Marteg to the hillslopes of Yr Wylorn to the north.

Fork right at a junction of paths, following signs for the Monks' Trod – the old route that connected the abbeys at Strata Florida and Abbeycwmhir. The green trod runs through a copse, turns right, uphill, just beyond a gate into a field and swings left to become a really excellent path on a terrace some way up the hillside. The

Built in the 1860s as part of an alternative route from South Wales to North West England, the line carried few passengers and only a little more freight traffic, and was an early casualty of the Beeching cuts in 1962.

route runs along a boardwalk for some distance, traverses a couple of hay meadows and goes through a field gate into a green lane, which then joins a tarmac lane just before the longhouse and visitor centre at **Gilfach**.

The path along the trackbed of the Mid Wales Railway

> **Gilfach** is a magnificent 168ha (416-acre) nature reserve owned by the Radnorshire Wildlife Trust and it is home to a huge variety of species, many of which face a fight for survival. The reserve is based around a classic 15th-century cruck-framed longhouse built into the hill, with living accommodation at the top end and a byre for the animals below. Across the courtyard an old barn is now used as a nature discovery centre.

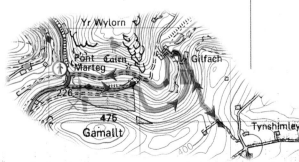

149

The cruck-framed longhouse at Gilfach

To extend the walk and savour the best of the views, take the path signposted to Tynshimley (and also as the Wye Valley Walk) from the courtyard between the barn and the longhouse, zigzagging above the farm on a stony track above woodland that provides a summer home for pied flycatchers and redstarts, and then, beyond a gate, rising across an immense field on a green path cut into the hill.

As height is gained the scenery becomes increasingly impressive, both westwards down the Marteg Valley to the forbidding cliffs of Cerrig Gwalch, and northwards across the valley to Pen-rhiw and the rounded hills of Drysgol and Pen Crwn. On reaching the ridge the views are even more extensive, now including the rolling hills to the east. Closer to hand, but not especially impressive, are the house platforms marked on the map, which hint at an earlier, more expansive, phase of human settlement here.

Return by the same route to the longhouse and take the tarmac access lane, swinging right to descend to and cross the river next to the otter hide. Take the grassy path immediately on the left, going through rough meadows just above the river that are favoured by green wood-peckers feeding on yellow ants. The path runs through a series of fields, passing a viewing point for a series of little waterfalls where spawning salmon can be seen attempting to leap the falls in autumn. ▶

The path climbs away from the river for a while and then drops back down to the water's edge, passing a deep pool once used by local farmers as a sheep wash. Shingle banks here provide a feeding ground for common sandpipers, while dippers and grey wagtails flit about the rocky pools and dragonflies and damselflies hover above the water.

Finally the path, still signposted as the nature trail, leaves the river and zigzags up to a junction of paths; just to the right is the entrance to the old Mid Wales Railway tunnel – now used as a hibernation site for bats and a roost for owls – but keep straight on here, signposted to Pont Marteg. The path rises gently, overlooking the boggy flood plain of the Marteg, then merges with the quiet valley road for the final 400m back to the car park near **Pont Marteg**, with a striking new sculpture on the right and a modern interpretation of a stone circle by the picnic area to the left.

The river here is also home to brown trout, chub, grayling and pike.

Waterfalls and salmon leaps on the Afon Marteg

151

WALK 28

The Monks' Trod

Start/Finish	Pont Marteg (SN 952 715)
Distance	13km (8 miles)
Ascent	420m (1380ft)
Time	4–5hrs
Map	Explorer 200
Public transport	Infrequent bus services between Rhayader and Aberystwyth or Llanidloes run via Pont Marteg
Parking	Large layby on the A470

This superb walk follows part of the medieval Monks' Trod, which ran between the abbeys of Abbeycwmhir and Strata Florida, before visiting two prehistoric standing stones and descending a wonderful green path into the Fergwm side-valley below the cliffs of Cerrig Gwalch.

From **Pont Marteg** a waymark post points the way to a path descending to a narrow wooden footbridge over the Wye – still a turbulent upland river here and particularly picturesque downstream from the bridge. Take the path

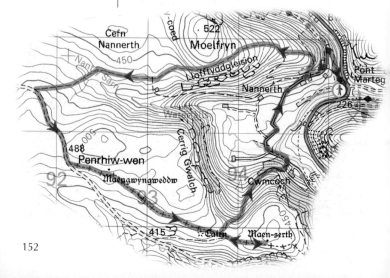

angling to the right and climbing through open woodland to reach and turn left on a narrow lane. The lane curves to the right and passes through a gate above Nannerth Fawr, now the centre of a tourism enterprise. However, the route bears right just before the gate, taking a signposted bridleway that climbs steadily through Coed Nannerth-fawr.

The way passes a seat with an excellent prospect eastwards across the Wye to the Marteg Valley and swings left to go through a gate. Head straight across a sloping field to a second gate, turn right and go through a third gate (another seat here has a great view too, southwards along the Wye) to reach the open moorland, now following a slightly sunken trackway on the line of the Monks' Trod.

Described as an 'ancient road' on generations of OS maps, the **Monks' Trod** crossed 24 miles (40km) of remote, desolate moorland between the abbeys of Strata Florida and Abbeycwmhir and was a high-quality route that could be covered in a day on horseback. Evidence of its construction survives in paved sections, bridge supports and parts of the route that are cut into the slope and embanked. It simply fell into disuse after the dissolution, and exists today as a challenging high-level mountain path.

The ruins of the summer dwelling at Lluest-pen-rhiw

The next part of the walk is magnificent, along a superb grassy path through bilberries, heather and gorse. The trod is clearly man-made, with traces of its construction visible in places, but it merges into the moorland landscape and is very easily followed across the rocky southern shoulder of **Moelfryn**. Beyond an unexpected waymark post (take the bridleway going slightly left here) there is a sudden dramatic view of the cliff-face of Cerrig Gwalch ahead and to the left. The path dips down slightly, crossing the boggy headwaters of the Trawsnant, and becomes less well defined as it passes close to the evocative ruins of the shepherd's cottage at Lluest-pen-rhiw. ◄

Around the ruined cottage there is a series of small fields with upright slate boundary stones on earthen banks.

The route is now crossing rough grassland, its course generally visible as a green track until it drops down stonily and damply past rocks to the monks' ford at Rhyd Garreg-lwyd. Below the crags a sheepfold lies on top of a late medieval longhouse sheltered by a now-ruined wall. The track then regains height across the moorland and reaches the mountain road between Rhayader and Aberystwyth. The Monks' Trod goes right here, down to Pont-ar-Elan, but instead turn left to follow the road for around 600m and then take a strikingly white stony track across the flanks of **Penrhiw-wen**, discovering the misshapen white quartzite standing stone of **Maengwyngweddw** on the left of the track after another few hundred metres. ◄

The 'white widow's stone' is small and squat, and undoubtedly prehistoric in origin, but it found a new lease of life as a waymarker for drovers travelling between Cwmystwyth and Rhayader.

Beyond Maengwyngweddw the prominent track continues across the plateau before dipping down past the Bronze Age **burial cairn** of Clap-yr-Arian, covered in bilberries, to a walker's crossroads close to a fenced-off area of subsidence. The route goes left here, steeply downhill, but before tackling the descent it is worth continuing along a green path climbing steadily up to the prominent standing stone of **Maen Serth**, high on the summit slopes of Esgair Dderw.

Over two metres high and with a badly worn incised cross on its eastern face, **Maen Serth** dates from the Bronze Age but achieved notoriety as the spot where Roger Mortimer ambushed and killed

the brothers Einion Clud and Cadwallon in the 12th century. Like Maengwyngweddw to the north-west, it was later used as a marker stone for routes across the mainly featureless Elenydd uplands.

The prehistoric standing stone of Maen Serth

Back at the crossroads of paths, turn right just beyond the fenced-off area, initially on a thin path but then on a really enjoyable green track dropping down through bilberry and then bracken, with the great wooded cliff of Cerrig Gwalch, defended by steep scree slopes, away to the left. ▶ This is a magnificent path, with wide views into and across the fertile valley and nothing but the sounds of wildlife to disturb the peace.

Ignore a path on the left that heads towards Fergwm – the centre of a small estate dating back to Elizabethan times – and contour below rocks, still on springy green turf. Go through a gate, almost immediately turn left through a second, and descend steeply through a classic Wye Valley oak wood to reach a very quiet country lane. Turn left, following the lane as it twists and turns just above the river, passing the Tudor longhouse at Nannerth Ganol (with cruck trusses, mullioned windows and tall chimney) and the old farmhouse at **Nannerth Fawr** before following the outward route back to the pedestrian bridge at **Pont Marteg** and its wonderful river scenery.

Cerrig Gwalch (Hawk Rock) supports a variety of breeding birds in the broadleaved woodland clinging to its slopes, while lily-of-the-valley and mountain melick are also found here.

WALK 29
Llangurig to Llanidloes

Start	Blue Bell Inn, Llangurig (SN 907 798)
Finish	Old Market Hall, Llanidloes (SN 953 844)
Distance	8km (5 miles)
Ascent	155m (510ft)
Time	3hrs
Map	Explorer 214
Public transport	Buses (principally the 525 and X75) run between Llanidloes and Llangurig roughly every two hours: leave the car in Llanidloes, take the bus to Llangurig and walk back to the car
Parking	Car parks and roadside parking in both Llangurig and Llanidloes

This is a pleasant walk with easy ridge walking and an excellent outlook over the Upper Wye and Severn valleys. The two rivers rise close together on the eastern flanks of Plynlimon, and even here, some 15km (around 10 miles) downstream, the journey from one river to the other is short and simple.

Pencroesau was formerly the home of a woman who earned a living as a fortune teller and claimed to cure sickness by using the mineral waters from a nearby spring.

The route leaves **Llangurig** – once an important droving centre but now a quiet upland village above the flood plain of the infant Wye – by taking the lane by the side of the Blue Bell Inn and climbing close to the site of Llangurig station on the ill-fated Manchester & Milford line. Continue uphill past the Methodist chapel, rebuilt in 1904 in an Arts and Crafts style, to reach Pencroesau. ◄ The lane gains height more steadily now, passing through a typical landscape of small fields around dispersed upland farms, eventually reaching a metalled bridleway that curves left and right before reaching the farm complex at **Pen-hyle-mawr**.

The **Manchester & Milford Railway** was authorised by Parliament to build a line from Llanidloes through Llangurig to Aberystwyth in 1860. The track was laid four years later and a passing loop installed at the proposed Llangurig station (the site of which can still be seen in a shallow rock cutting above the village) but no buildings or other facilities were completed, and only a single freight train ever ran along the route. The line was dismantled in 1882 and the rails reused elsewhere.

Bear left on the bridleway through the farm buildings and left again to follow the waymarked track across two large fields, then bear right through a gate into a little lane that leads down to a bridge over the outflow from **Marsh's Pool**. ▶ The way lies past an archetypal example of a Welsh upland farmhouse at Glan-y-rhyd, then across fields to reach a forestry plantation. The track scythes through the conifers, drops down the damp and steep-sided upper valley of the Afon Dulas and then keeps to the left-hand hedge-line across a series of fields towards **Cefn-y-bwlch Farm**, with good views ahead of the field-scape around Llanidloes in the upper Severn valley.

The bridleway continues ahead, keeping to the crest of the broad declining ridge across the wooded slopes

A delightful upland lake in a shallow wooded hollow, Marsh's Pool was dammed to provide a reliable water supply for local farms.

Cefn-y-bwlch and the wooded slopes of Allt y Gofau

A fish pass has been built by the weir at Felindre Mill to allow returning salmon and eels to access the upper Severn.

The friary was built as recently as 1951 and commemorates Richard Gwyn – a native of Llanidloes who became the first Catholic martyr in Wales when he was executed in Wrexham in 1584.

of Allt y Gofau. Leave the wood through a gate, aiming diagonally left across a big oblong field to find a lane at the far left corner. Take the lane to a bridge across a stream, turn right and follow the stream until the track turns left to emerge on a country road just above Felindre Bridge, with the site of the 19th-century Felindre Mill away to the left. ◄

Keep right to cross the bridge and take Penygreen Road towards the market town of Llanidloes, passing the Franciscan friary. ◄ Turn right across the Short Bridge, with the former Bridgend flannel and corn mills immediately to the right and Highgate Terrace, with its open weaving loft and adjacent disused town gaol, abutting the bridge to the left.

Llanidloes was granted its charter in 1280 but was at its most prosperous from the 17th to 19th centuries, when the textile trade in the town supported a series of flannel mills powered by steam and water, while the area to the north-west of the town was an important lead-mining centre.

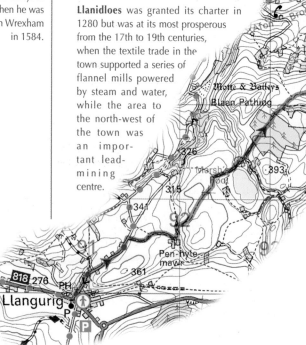

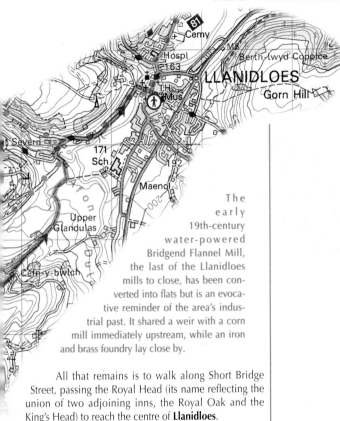

The early 19th-century water-powered Bridgend Flannel Mill, the last of the Llanidloes mills to close, has been converted into flats but is an evocative reminder of the area's industrial past. It shared a weir with a corn mill immediately upstream, while an iron and brass foundry lay close by.

All that remains is to walk along Short Bridge Street, passing the Royal Head (its name reflecting the union of two adjoining inns, the Royal Oak and the King's Head) to reach the centre of **Llanidloes**.

Right at the town's central crossroads is the only remaining half-timbered **market hall** in Powys, its ground floor mostly open to the elements, with substantial oak arches and cobbled paving. The upper room was variously used as a wool market, a law court, a Working Men's Institute & Library and a preacher's hall, used by John Wesley and other notable clerics.

159

WALK 30
Plynlimon and the source of the Wye

Start/Finish	Eisteddfa Gurig (SN 797 840)
Distance	15km (9½ miles)
Ascent	540m (1770ft)
Time	4–6hrs
Maps	Explorer 213, 214
Public transport	Buses X47 and 525 provide an infrequent service from Aberystwyth to Llanidloes or Rhayader, passing through Eisteddfa Gurig
Parking	Car park (honesty box) at Eisteddfa Gurig farmhouse

This is an exhilarating mountain expedition that includes an ascent of Plynlimon (Pumlumon Fawr), at 752m (2467ft) the highest mountain in Mid Wales. It traverses a bleak moorland region that can be an acquired taste, but the going is easy and the sense of space infectious.

The route to the hills zigzags up through the farm buildings at **Eisteddfa Gurig** to go through a gate (helpfully labelled 'all paths') and swing left on a broad, stony miners' track with the Afon Tarennig and its little cascades down to the right. The track curves right, gaining height gradually and uneventfully as it passes a redundant stile, with the substantial remains of the Pumlumon mine gradually coming into view ahead, backed by the whaleback of Pen Lluest-y-carn – Plynlimon's south-eastern outlier.

The **Pumlumon mine** opened in 1867 and yielded over 3000 tons of lead concentrates over little more than a decade, but it flooded in 1878 and was only worked sporadically thereafter, closing for good in 1897. It was entirely water-powered, with two massive waterwheels, and worked using a combination of adits (levels driven into the hill) and vertical shafts. The extensive remains include the wheel pits, old mine buildings and ugly spoil heaps.

One of the wheel pits at the Pumlumon mine

Immediately beyond the mine workings a signpost indicates the point at which the Plynlimon path leaves the track along the Tarennig valley. The path, stony at first, goes to the left here as it climbs steadily through featureless rough grassland, with a good retrospective view of the Tarennig valley and the rounded hills of Mid Wales, increasingly dominated by the substantial Cefn Croes wind farm. The path becomes increasingly stony, and one or two venerable wooden posts help with route-finding, with Plynlimon's summit plateau ahead and to the left and the headwaters of the Afon Tarennig down to the right; further to the right there is a superb view down the Wye Valley towards Llangurig.

The last stage of the ascent has much more of a mountain feel to it, with the course of the path shown by increasingly frequent wooden posts and then by stone cairns as it negotiates little crags and boulder fields.

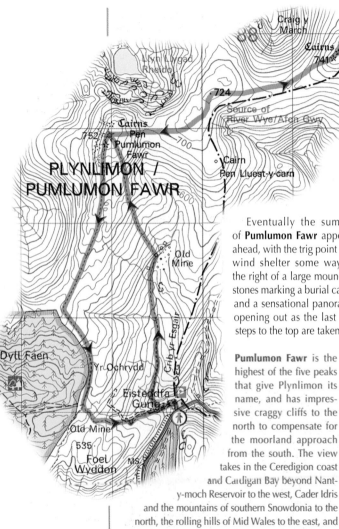

Eventually the summit of **Pumlumon Fawr** appears ahead, with the trig point and wind shelter some way to the right of a large mound of stones marking a burial cairn, and a sensational panorama opening out as the last few steps to the top are taken.

Pumlumon Fawr is the highest of the five peaks that give Plynlimon its name, and has impressive craggy cliffs to the north to compensate for the moorland approach from the south. The view takes in the Ceredigion coast and Cardigan Bay beyond Nant-y-moch Reservoir to the west, Cader Idris and the mountains of southern Snowdonia to the north, the rolling hills of Mid Wales to the east, and the unmistakable skyline of the Brecon Beacons to the south.

To find the source of the river Wye turn east at the summit and follow the fence down towards a prominent cairn in the col below. A boggy area and some peat hags impede progress for a while, but the Lluest-y-carn ridge, marked by a cairn and slate boundary stone in close proximity, is easily gained. An obvious path now leads across the plateau towards Pen Pumlumon Arwystli, but to get to the source of the Wye it is necessary to clamber over the fence to the right and drop down into a steeply shelving valley, with the source defended by spongy, uneven clumps of rough grass. ▶

Return to the main path and turn right, rising steadily up the south-western slopes of **Pen Pumlumon Arwystli**, possibly the most scenic of the Plynlimon tops and certainly with the most significant prehistoric associations. Three prominent Bronze Age burial mounds, each of

The untrodden upper valley is unspectacular but leads the eye down the course of the river to Hafren Forest and the green Cwmdeuddwr hills.

The summit of Plynlimon, looking west to Nant-y-moch reservoir and Cardigan Bay

*The valley of the
Afon Tarennig above
Eisteddfa Gurig*

A classic mountain
tarn in a deep
corrie gouged out
by glacial ice, Llyn
Lhygad Rheidol
has been enlarged
and dammed as a
reservoir but is still
highly scenic.

them now hollowed out to form effective wind shelters, adorn the summit plateau. The view back to the top of Plynlimon is excellent, as is the eastward prospect over the upper Severn valley and Hafren Forest, but to complete the walk it is necessary to return to the summit of Plynlimon, using the same path across the plateau but diverging north of the cairns to gain the best views down into the deep basin containing Llyn Lhygad Rheidol. ◄

Go back over the ladder stile at the summit and turn right, dropping gently down the south ridge (Pen y Drawsallt) on rough grass with some heather providing welcome colour. The best line lies just to the east of a fence, past a couple of ponds and along the rocky crest of the ridge, with rolling green hills to the left and Nant y Moch Reservoir to the right. The path is well defined until it passes through a gap in the fence and becomes less easy to follow – although the direction of travel is obvious, still following the fence, which is now on the left. The subsidiary summit of Y Garn, itself a fine viewpoint, is away to the right, with the edge of the Dyll Faen conifer plantation appearing to block the way ahead.

Eventually a thin path materialises, leading to another gap in the fence and to a broad stony track that leads round to the right, dropping down with the forest edge on the right and the Cefn Croes wind farm straight ahead. Beyond a stile a little stream, the Nant Nod, joins from the left and the descent continues, eventually swinging left where a bridleway comes in over a stile from the right. The key is to remain on the stony track as it meanders down below the slopes of **Yr Ochrydd**, passing the remains of more mine workings somewhat overshadowed by a massive modern barn. ▸ The track then runs high above the Afon Tarennig to go through a gate and rejoin the outward route, turning right to weave through the farm buildings at **Eisteddfa Gurig** and return to the car park.

The lead mine at Yr Ochrydd closed in the late 19th century and is now represented by spoil heaps and the foundations of buildings close to the stream.

APPENDIX A

Route summary table

Walk	Title	Start/Finish	Distance	Ascent	Time	Map	Page
The Lower Wye Chepstow to Ross-on-Wye							
1	The Lancaut Peninsula	Rising Sun, Woodcroft (ST 542 957)	5km (3 miles)	110m (360ft)	2hrs	Outdoor Leisure 14	28
2	The Wyndcliff	Lower Wyndcliff car park (ST 526 971)	7km (4½ miles)	175m (575ft)	2–3hrs	Outdoor Leisure 14	32
3	The Devil's Pulpit from the east	The Park, Tidenham Chase (ST 993 558)	6km (4 miles)	90m (295ft)	2hrs	Outdoor Leisure 14	36
4	Tintern and the Angidy Valley	Tintern Abbey (SO 533 002)	11km (7 miles)	290m (950ft)	3–5hrs	Outdoor Leisure 14	40
5	Trellech and Beacon Hill	Trellech Church (SO 500 055)	12km (7½ miles)	310m (1015ft)	4–5hrs	Outdoor Leisure 14	45
6	The Kymin	White Horse, Staunton (SO 547 126)	8km (5 miles)	440m (1445ft)	3–4hrs	Outdoor Leisure 14	50
7	King Arthur's Cave and the Seven Sisters	Entrance to White Rocks Nature Reserve (SO 548 157)	7km (4½ miles)	220m (720ft)	2–3hrs	Outdoor Leisure 14	55
8	Coppet Hill and Goodrich	Goodrich Castle car park (SO 575 196)	12km (7½ miles)	235m (770ft)	3–5hrs	Outdoor Leisure 14	59

Walk	Title	Start/Finish	Distance	Ascent	Time	Map	Page
The Middle Wye: Ross-on-Wye to Hay-on-Wye							
9	Sellack and Hoarwithy	Hoarwithy Church (SO 545 294)	8km (5 miles)	105m (345ft)	2–3hrs	Explorer 189	66
10	Capler Camp from Fownhope	Fownhope recreation ground (SO 578 341)	10km (6 miles)	315m (1035ft)	3–4hrs	Explorer 189	70
11	Haugh Wood	Forestry Commission car park (SO 592 365)	8km (5 miles)	190m (620ft)	3hrs	Explorer 189	75
12	Aconbury Hill	Little Birch village hall (SO 505 324)	11km (7 miles)	260m (855ft)	3–4hrs	Explorer 189	79
13	Breinton Springs	High Town, Hereford (SO 510 400)	12km (7½ miles)	50m (165ft)	3–4hrs	Explorer 189	84
14	Black and White Weobley	Weobley Church (SO 401 518)	7km (4½ miles)	105m (345ft)	2–3hrs	Explorer 201, 202	88
15	Arthur's Stone and Merbach Common	Bredwardine Bridge (SO 336 446)	11km (7 miles)	290m (950ft)	3–4hrs	Outdoor Leisure 13	92
16	Kilvert's Clyro	Hay-on-Wye Buttermarket (SO 229 424)	10km (6 miles)	260m (855ft)	3–4hrs	Outdoor Leisure 13	97

Walk	Title	Start/Finish	Distance	Ascent	Time	Map	Page
Upper Middle Wye: Hay-on-Wye to Newbridge-on-Wye							
17	Talgarth and Llanelieu	Talgarth Mill (SO 154 336)	9km (6 miles)	285m (935ft)	3–4hrs	Outdoor Leisure 13	102
18	The Begwns	Cattle grid above Croesfeilliog (SO 181 445)	7km (4½ miles)	175m (575ft)	2–3hrs	Explorer 188 or Outdoor Leisure 13	106
19	Brechfa Pool	Boughrood Bridge (SO 130 384)	10km (6 miles)	450m (1475ft)	3–4hrs	Explorer 188	110
20	Llewellyn's Cave and Aberedw Rocks	Seven Stars, Aberedw (SO 080 472)	8km (5 miles)	290m (950ft)	2–3hrs	Explorer 188	115
21	Llandeilo Hill and Twm Tobacco's Grave	Seven Stars, Aberedw (SO 080 472)	12km (7½ miles)	510m (1675ft)	4–5hrs	Explorer 188	119
22	Builth and Banc-y-Celyn	Lion Hotel, Builth Wells (SO 042 510)	14km (9 miles)	495m (1625ft)	4–6hrs	Explorer 188	124
23	Cors y Llyn	Cors y Llyn car park (SO 015 557)	8km (5 miles)	110m (360ft)	2–3hrs	Explorer 200	129
24	Shaky Bridge	Shaky Bridge (SO 084 612)	12km (7½ miles)	420m (1380ft)	3–4hrs	Explorer 200	134

Walk	Title	Start/Finish	Distance	Ascent	Time	Map	Page
The Upper Wye: Newbridge-on-Wye to Plynlimon							
25	Above the Elan Valley reservoirs	North end of Garreg-ddu Reservoir (SN 915 673)	12km (7½ miles)	435m (1425ft)	3–4hrs	Explorer 200	140
26	Drygarn Fawr	Llanerch Cawr (SN 900 616)	15km (9½ miles)	460m (1510ft)	4–6hrs	Explorer 200	144
27	Gilfach Farm	Marteg Bridge car park (SN 953 714)	6km (3½ miles)	180m (590ft)	2hrs	Explorer 200	148
28	The Monks' Trod	Pont Marteg (SN 952 715)	13km (8 miles)	420m (1380ft)	4–5hrs	Explorer 200	152
29	Llangurig to Llanidloes	Start: Blue Bell Inn, Llangurig (SN 907 798); Finish: Old Market Hall, Llanidloes (SN 953 844)	8km (5 miles)	155m (510ft)	3hrs	Explorer 214	156
30	Plynlimon and the source of the Wye	Eisteddfa Gurig (SN 797 840)	15km (9½ miles)	540m (1770ft)	4–6hrs	Explorer 213, 214	160

APPENDIX B
Useful contacts

Local authorities

Gloucestershire County Council
01452 427614
www.gloucestershire.gov.uk

Forest of Dean District Council
01594 810000
www.fdean.gov.uk

Monmouthshire Council
01633 644644
www.monmouthshire.gov.uk

Herefordshire Council
01432 260500
www.herefordshire.gov.uk

Powys County Council
01597 827460
www.powys.gov.uk

Tourist information centres

Chepstow
Bridge Street
Chepstow
Monmouthshire
NP16 5EY
01291 623772
www.chepstow.co.uk

Tintern
The Old Station
Tintern
Monmouthshire
NP16 7NX
01291 689566
www.tinternvillage.co.uk

Monmouth
Shire Hall
Agincourt Square
Monmouth

Monmouthshire
NP5 3DY
01600 775257
www.monmouth.org.uk

Ross-on-Wye
Swan House
Edde Cross Street
Ross-on-Wye
Herefordshire
HR9 7BZ
01989 562768
www.rossonwye.com

Hereford
1 King Street
Hereford
Herefordshire
HR4 9BW
01432 268430
www.visitherefordshire.co.uk

Hay-on-Wye
Oxford Road
Hay-on-Wye
Herefordshire
HR3 5DG
01497 820144
www.hay-on-wye.co.uk

Llandrindod Wells
Town Hall
Temple Street
Llandrindod Wells
Powys
01597 822600
www.llandrindod.co.uk

Elan Valley
Elan Village
Rhayader
Powys
LD6 5HP
01597 810880
www.elanvalley.org.uk

Accommodation and local information

For the lower valley
Forest of Dean and Wye Valley AONB
0845 053 1173
www.wyedeantourism.co.uk

For the area between Goodrich and Hay-on-Wye
Visit Herefordshire & The Wye Valley
01432 268430
www.visitherefordshire.co.uk

For the Powys area
Visit Wales
0800 328 1000
www.visitwales.com

Explore Mid Wales
01597 827460
www.tourism.powys.gov.uk

The Wye Valley Walk
www.wyevalleywalk.org

Also the official guidebook to *The Wye Valley Walk* by the Wye Valley Walk Partnership (Cicerone, 2011)

Public transport

Train
National Rail
08457 484950
www.nationalrail.co.uk

Arriva Trains Wales
08457 484950
www.arrivatrainswales.co.uk

Bus
Powys, Herefordshire and Monmouthshire councils provide excellent information on their websites (listed above) for bus services in their area, while Gloucestershire redirects enquiries to the Traveline website (www.travelinesw.com).

LISTING OF CICERONE GUIDES

BRITISH ISLES CHALLENGES, COLLECTIONS AND ACTIVITIES

The End to End Trail
The Mountains of England and Wales: 1&2
The National Trails
The Relative Hills of Britain
The Ridges of England, Wales and Ireland
The UK Trailwalker's Handbook
The UK's County Tops
Three Peaks, Ten Tors

UK CYCLING

20 Classic Sportive Rides
  South West England
  South East England
Border Country Cycle Routes
Cycling in the Cotswolds
Cycling in the Hebrides
Cycling in the Peak District
Cycling in the Yorkshire Dales
Cycling the Pennine Bridleway
Mountain Biking in the Lake District
Mountain Biking in the Yorkshire Dales
Mountain Biking on the North Downs
Mountain Biking on the South Downs
The C2C Cycle Route
The End to End Cycle Route
The Lancashire Cycleway

SCOTLAND

Backpacker's Britain
  Central and Southern Scottish Highlands
  Northern Scotland
Ben Nevis and Glen Coe
Great Mountain Days in Scotland
Not the West Highland Way
Scotland's Best Small Mountains
Scotland's Far West
Scotland's Mountain Ridges
Scrambles in Lochaber
The Ayrshire and Arran Coastal Paths
The Border Country
The Cape Wrath Trail
The Great Glen Way
The Isle of Mull
The Isle of Skye

The Pentland Hills
The Skye Trail
The Southern Upland Way
The Speyside Way
The West Highland Way
Walking Highland Perthshire
Walking in Scotland's Far North
Walking in the Angus Glens
Walking in the Cairngorms
Walking in the Ochils, Campsie Fells and Lomond Hills
Walking in the Southern Uplands
Walking in Torridon
Walking Loch Lomond and the Trossachs
Walking on Harris and Lewis
Walking on Jura, Islay and Colonsay
Walking on Rum and the Small Isles
Walking on the Isle of Arran
Walking on the Orkney and Shetland Isles
Walking on Uist and Barra
Walking the Corbetts
  1 South of the Great Glen
  2 North of the Great Glen
Walking the Galloway Hills
Walking the Lowther Hills
Walking the Munros
  1 Southern, Central and Western Highlands
  2 Northern Highlands and the Cairngorms
Winter Climbs Ben Nevis and Glen Coe
Winter Climbs in the Cairngorms
World Mountain Ranges: Scotland

NORTHERN ENGLAND TRAILS

A Northern Coast to Coast Walk
Hadrian's Wall Path
The Dales Way
The Pennine Way

NORTH EAST ENGLAND, YORKSHIRE DALES AND PENNINES

Great Mountain Days in the Pennines
Historic Walks in North Yorkshire
South Pennine Walks
St Oswald's Way and St Cuthbert's Way

The Cleveland Way and the Yorkshire Wolds Way
The North York Moors
The Reivers Way
The Teesdale Way
The Yorkshire Dales
  North and East
  South and West
Walking in County Durham
Walking in Northumberland
Walking in the North Pennines
Walks in Dales Country
Walks in the Yorkshire Dales
Walks on the North York Moors – Books 1 & 2

NORTH WEST ENGLAND AND THE ISLE OF MAN

Historic Walks in Cheshire
Isle of Man Coastal Path
The Isle of Man
The Lune Valley and Howgills
The Ribble Way
Walking in Cumbria's Eden Valley
Walking in Lancashire
Walking in the Forest of Bowland and Pendle
Walking on the West Pennine Moors
Walks in Lancashire Witch Country
Walks in Ribble Country
Walks in Silverdale and Arnside
Walks in the Forest of Bowland

LAKE DISTRICT

Coniston Copper Mines
Great Mountain Days in the Lake District
Lake District: High Fell Walks
Lake District: Low Level and Lake Walks
Lake District Winter Climbs
Lakeland Fellranger
  The Central Fells
  The Far-Eastern Fells
  The Mid-Western Fells
  The Near Eastern Fells
  The Northern Fells
  The North-Western Fells
  The Southern Fells
  The Western Fells
Roads and Tracks of the Lake District
Rocky Rambler's Wild Walks

For full information on all our
guides, books and eBooks,
visit our website:
www.cicerone.co.uk.

Walking – Trekking – Mountaineering – Climbing – Cycling

Over 40 years, Cicerone have built up an outstanding collection of 300 guides, inspiring all sorts of amazing adventures.

Every guide comes from extensive exploration and research by our expert authors, all with a passion for their subjects. They are frequently praised, endorsed and used by clubs, instructors and outdoor organisations.

All our titles can now be bought as **e-books** and many as iPad and Kindle files and we will continue to make all our guides available for these and many other devices.

Our website shows any **new information** we've received since a book was published. Please do let us know if you find anything has changed, so that we can pass on the latest details. On our **website** you'll also find some great ideas and lots of information, including sample chapters, contents lists, reviews, articles and a photo gallery.

It's easy to keep in touch with what's going on at Cicerone, by getting our monthly **free e-newsletter**, which is full of offers, competitions, up-to-date information and topical articles. You can subscribe on our home page and also follow us on **Facebook** and **Twitter**, as well as our **blog**.

Cicerone – the very best guides for exploring the world.

CICERONE

2 Police Square Milnthorpe Cumbria LA7 7PY
Tel: 015395 62069 info@cicerone.co.uk
www.cicerone.co.uk